BRICS OR BUST?

Escaping the Middle-Income Trap

HARTMUT ELSENHANS

AND SALVATORE BABONES

stanford briefs
An Imprint of Stanford University Press
Stanford, California

Stanford University Press
Stanford, California

©2017 by the Board of Trustees of the
Leland Stanford Junior University.

Printed in the United States of America
on acid-free, archival-quality paper

Library of Congress Cataloging-in-Publication Data

Names: Elsenhans, Hartmut, 1941– author. | Babones, Salvatore J., author.
Title: BRICS or bust? : escaping the middle-income trap / Hartmut
    Elsenhans and Salvatore Babones.
Description: Stanford, California : Stanford Briefs, an imprint of Stanford
    University Press, 2017. | Includes bibliographical references.
Identifiers: LCCN 2017022244 (print) | LCCN 2017026896 (ebook) |
    ISBN 9780804799898 (pbk. : alk. paper) | ISBN 9781503604919 (ebook)
Subjects: LCSH: BRIC countries—Economic conditions. | BRIC
    countries—Economic policy.
Classification: LCC HC59.7 (ebook) | LCC HC59.7 .E455 2017 (print) |
    DDC 330.9172/4—dc23

LC record available at https://lccn.loc.gov/2017022244

Typeset by Classic Typography in 10/13 Adobe Garamond

CONTENTS

PREFACE AND ACKNOWLEDGMENTS

From a sheer human standpoint, the BRICS countries are among the most important in the world, accounting for 40 percent of the world's population and standing symbolically for the hopes and dreams of many more. Through good policy choices they can avoid or escape the middle-income trap, and we hope that they will. This book offers them, and countries like them, a clear path to prosperity. We sincerely hope that they will chose it.

That this book exists is a practical testament to the importance of students in the intellectual development of their professors. We were first introduced to each other in August 2014 by a former student of Hartmut's. Daniel Kremers of the German Institute for Japanese Studies had attended one of Salvatore's lectures, where he spoke of Hartmut and described him as "mind blowing and entertaining." Two and a half years later, Salvatore must concur. We can only hope that this book is mind blowing and entertaining as well. For this would be a good sign that it will have an impact in the world!

We will keep our acknowledgments to a minimum. But we must thank our editor at Stanford University Press, Margo Beth Fleming, for believing in this project enough to suffer us through several long delays. We are also grateful to her for providing detailed editorial feedback that greatly improved the final text. We would also like to thank Professors Samuel Cohn, Robert Holton, and Ray Kiely for their comments and advice. Finally, we are grateful to the copy editor, Jeff Wyneken, who produced the final, polished typescript, for his careful reading.

Hartmut Elsenhans, *Leipzig*
Salvatore Babones, *Sydney*
April 20, 2017

BRICS OR BUST?

INTRODUCTION

The rise and fall of Brazil, Russia, India, and China, the so-called BRIC nations, is the great geoeconomic story of the twenty-first century. In the early 2000s, these countries were tipped to redraw the economic map of the world. With a combined population of nearly three billion, they constituted roughly 40 percent of the world's people. Throughout the first decade of the new millennium, they were among the fastest-growing countries in the world, sailing through the 2008–9 global financial crisis in a way that made them the envy of the world. When the long-standing G-7 group of developed countries proved unable to meet the challenges posed by the crisis, the wider G-20—including all four BRIC economies—rose to the occasion. At a time when developed countries were talking austerity, the BRIC countries opened the taps on government spending. The crisis did not turn into the second Great Depression (though it looked as though it might in early 2009). For this, surely some of the credit goes to the swift action taken by the BRICs to stimulate domestic demand.

Fast-forward a few years and the BRICs seem a spent force. Brazil is facing a political crisis of momentous proportions as it deals with its second year of recession. Russia's economy is also stagnating under the combined pressures of low oil prices, Western sanctions, and incessant military action. India, much poorer than the other BRICs, is the lone economic bright spot—but clouds are gathering and even the Reserve Bank of India believes that its growth is unsustainable. And then there's China. In theory, China is the engine of the global economy, continuing to grow at more than 6 percent per year despite the fact that it is now a middle-income country and the world's second-largest economy. In practice, there are grave doubts about the veracity of China's economic statistics. In late January 2016, after a run of bad economic news, China removed the director of its National Bureau of Statistics for "violating party discipline." China's economic statistics improved dramatically immediately following the appointment of a new director in early March.

The role of the BRIC countries in the global economy may at times be overstated, but there is no denying their importance—both as economies and as examples. In the popular imagination, the BRICs have made the transition from acronym to model. China in particular has become the articulation of the global economy: neither the consumer nor the producer of last resort but the place where demand and supply meet to cater to the world's needs and desires. China is the great crossroads, the focal point of the world's manufacturing supply chains, a position it occupied before Europe's industrial revolution and has come to occupy again. Brazil and Russia have long been middle-income countries and have experienced many episodes of rising hopes followed by long-term stagnation. Besides, both are primarily resource-based economies, not models of industrial upgrading. India is growing rapidly but is still a very poor country, more a BRIC of the future than a BRIC of today.

If the BRICs do not provide a single, exportable growth model that can be copied by other developing countries, their experiences can at least teach lessons that can be learned, point to pitfalls that can be avoided, and offer hope that better economies (and better societies) are within reach for countries that are sufficiently well governed to pursue them. In a recent book review in *Foreign Affairs,* political scientist Nicolas van de Walle wrote of a particular country that "Greedy national elites have always preferred to appropriate public resources for their private use rather than grow the national economy or govern effectively." No economic policy can solve the problem of greedy national elites. But even development-minded elites lack disinterested guidance as to what specific policies could help their countries rise out of the middle income levels of the global economy. If national elites are to be expected to make real personal sacrifices today for the future good of their countries, they should at least be given good reasons to believe that their sacrifices will not be in vain. The BRIC examples are not promising in this regard. But their experiences do light some paths forward.

Economists and other social scientists have assembled quite a lot of evidence about how poor countries can reach middle-income status. Most of the required interventions involve the removal of supply-side bottlenecks: a modern economy requires a literate workforce, the liberation of women, basic transportation networks, decent public health, and the provision of a minimum level of law and order. As first China and now India have demonstrated, the introduction of market forces can liberate economies that were previously held down by bad central planning, but as Russia and Brazil have demonstrated, market forces do not necessarily produce better outcomes than can be achieved by even mediocre central planning. Supply-side good governance is surely a good thing in itself, but it takes only moderately competent levels of public administration to raise an economy from poor to middle income levels of productivity. Just look at Mexico, which has been stuck in the middle of the middle-income range for as long as economic statistics have been kept.

There is much less evidence about how middle-income countries can attain high income levels. Evidence is hard to come by in part because only one large country has ever unequivocally accomplished this feat. In the 1930s, Japan was a middle-income country that was economically and socially similar in many ways to today's rapidly industrializing countries of central and eastern Europe. Its brutal military expansionism was remarkable, but not its economic productivity. Then between 1950 and 1990, Japan rose to become one of the richest countries in the world. This required—or at least was accompanied by—massive demand-side changes in the structure of the Japanese economy: much higher levels of domestic consumption, much higher levels of government spending, the democratization of income and wealth, policies to promote full employment, and (fundamentally) the redirection of the benefits of economic growth away from national elites in favor of ordinary consumers.

Not coincidentally, these are all structural changes that the leading economies of the West experienced a generation or two earlier. As a late developer, Japan employed different strategies to achieve these objectives, but it ended up with an economy that is very similar to those of the developed West. Like Japan, today's middle-income countries will also formulate their own distinctive strategies for development, but as with Japan the structural impacts of those strategies will depend on the expansion of mass consumption. Japan may have experienced more than two decades of economic malaise since the early 1990s, but its people still enjoy one of the highest living standards in the world. Leading Western economists like Larry Summers correctly identify a lack of consumer demand as the root cause of the stagnation that currently afflicts nearly all of the world's high-income countries outside North America. In other words, today's high-income countries are slowly drifting toward middle-income status because people are not buying enough to continue to propel them ahead. It takes only a slight shift in vantage point to reveal that a lack of demand is also what keeps middle-income countries from rising toward high-income status.

AGING TIGER, FLYING GOOSE

The way that the BRIC nations came together as a cohort is now well known. In a 2001 investment research report, industry economist Jim O'Neill coined the term "BRIC" to describe the four large emerging market economies of Brazil, Russia, India, and China. These BRIC countries began meeting as a group in the mid-2000s to coordinate economic policies and lobby for greater representation in intergovernmental organizations. After an intense bout of lobbying, the BRICs became the "BRICSs" with the admission of South Africa into the formal summit system among these countries in 2010. Though South Africa is much smaller than the other BRICSs in the overall size of its population and economy, it is similar to them in national income per capita and overall economic structure. Like Russia and Brazil its economy is highly dependent on natural resources, and like all of the BRICs, it has extraordinarily high levels of income inequality. It also gives the BRICSs an outpost in Africa, making the group more globally representative.

In 2011 O'Neill began to promote the "next eleven" emerging market economies, from which he later carved out the MINTs (Mexico, Indonesia, Nigeria, Turkey). Acronym groupings like the BRICs, BRICSs, and MINTs that pull together the largest emerging market economies are mainly of interest to businesses and investors, people for whom market size matters. They are less useful for driving policies to promote growth, since sheer size tends to be uncorrelated with economic, political, and social indicators that policymakers care about. Still, they do serve to focus attention—and they do have the potential to promote global policy change.

Much has been spoken of a new BRICS economic model of state-led development, but little of it is new. Careful followers of development debates may remember a previous era's acronym, the NICs (newly industrialized countries). The original NICs were the four "Asian tigers" of Hong Kong, Singapore, South Korea, and Taiwan, though the term later came to be applied more expansively. Just like today's BRICSs, all four NICs had (and have) very large state sectors. Thus one obvious lesson that can be learned from the NICs is that a large state sector is no barrier to development; after all, much of Singapore's domestic economy is state owned. Many other lessons can be learned as well. Perhaps the biggest is that development can spill over from country to country as foreign investment and domestic pro-growth policies spread across borders (or in the case of East Asia, oceans). The spread of industrialization from Japan to the NICs and finally to China is known as the "flying geese" model of development. The biggest foreign investors in China today are not from Western countries. They are from the NICs.

The NICs may have been enormously successful, but they do not provide full-scale development models that can be copied by the BRICs. To begin with, Singapore and Hong Kong are central cities that are (statistically) separated from their respective geographical hinterlands. Taiwan benefited enormously from a massive influx of (relatively) skilled refugees after the end of China's civil war in 1949. The economies of Hong Kong and Singapore were similarly boosted by very large influxes of skilled refugees from China and Indonesia. South Korea, the one remaining Asian tiger NIC, also exhibits some unique qualities. Its geography and its history place it between the historical success of Japan and a (now) rapidly rising China. South Korea's success has depended as much on its lucky geographical location as on any policies of its own. Korea's historical misfortune (to be caught between the two Asian giants of China and Taiwan) has turned out to be its modern economic salvation.

China is the only one of the BRICS countries that has benefited from "flying geese"-style economic growth, and even in China this has been mostly limited to the coastal provinces that surround Hong Kong and Shanghai: the Pearl River Delta and the

Yangtze River Delta. The rest of China has been left to develop by its own devices, and has been much less successful. The northeastern Dongbei region and the interior western provinces of China are depopulating as hundreds of millions of migrant workers head toward the coast. As China's growth slows to a crawl in the mid-2010s, it is pulling the other Asian tigers down with it. It's as if the flying geese have all turned around to fly home.

China is at least closely tied into global economic networks through its integration into the East Asian economic sphere. The other BRICS countries, by contrast, are much more isolated from the larger global economy. Their companies are not closely integrated into global production networks and thus their people have few opportunities to upgrade their positions in global value chains. And like China, the other three original BRICs are too large to be pulled out of middle-income status by big wins in particular industries. The four small NIC economies could be completely transformed by the success of important export industries, like shipbuilding (Korea) or semiconductors (Taiwan). The BRICs are too big for that. They need domestic development, not just export success.

THE MIDDLE-INCOME "TRAP"

The economist James Heckman has written that policy questions fall into three types: problems of internal validity, problems of external validity, and ... more-difficult problems. Internal validation problems require only an evaluation of whether or not a specific policy worked at a specific time in a specific place. Did China's massive infrastructure spending in 2009 stimulate growth? Yes, certainly. External validation problems call for a forecast of the effects of a specific policy in a new environment. Would a 2009 China–style infrastructure stimulus have boosted growth in 2015 Russia? Maybe. But most policy questions fall into a third category of anticipating the effects of policies that have never actually been tried before in quite the same form. Building mass transit systems provided a short-term boost in China in 2009; would building housing provide a long-term boost in Russia in 2020? That is an altogether more difficult question.

The only way to answer (or make a good-faith attempt to answer) these kinds of challenging economic policy questions is to use economic theory to unpack the available evidence drawn from policies that have been tried in the past and reassemble it in ways that make sense for the formulation of policies for the future. The BRICS countries offer ample scope for this. They may have massive problems, but they have also scored massive successes. They may not have reached high income status, but they have at least overcome most of the supply-side challenges that keep other countries stuck at low-income levels. And they seem to have the administrative capacity to undertake ambitious reform programs once an elite consensus is reached on the right direction forward. When it comes to breaking out of the middle-income trap, they may yet surprise. But will they succeed?

The economics of growth and development is chock-full of traps of all kinds and descriptions. At its most straightforward, the idea of the middle-income trap is based on a simple observation: many countries have moved back and forth between the lower- and middle-income tiers of the global economy, but relatively few countries have moved back and forth between the middle and upper tiers. It is more a barrier than a trap: it is true that middle-income countries rarely move up, but it is equally true that high-income countries rarely move down. In a nutshell, the thesis presented in this book is that *the ceiling for middle-income countries is caused by the inequalities that are typically generated early in the development process itself.* An insufficient expansion of mass consumption shifts middle-income economies toward an emphasis on luxury goods, while profits are disproportionately captured by elites. High-income countries with strong civil societies are prevented from falling down the global income hierarchy by politics that favor mass consumption, but middle-income countries with weak civil societies have trouble getting over the political hurdles to continued growth in mass incomes.

Leaving aside exceptional cases like Japan and the NICs, few countries have ever risen from middle to high-income status. Some countries have temporarily become rich due to massive natural resource endowments (e.g., Kuwait), but essentially they are not really high-income countries. That is to say, they do not possess economic systems that generate high income levels for the participants in them. They are merely rentier states, prone to economic collapse if the world ever loses interest in their one product. The most extreme example of this is the Pacific island state of Nauru. Once the guano capital of the world, it was put out of business by the Haber-Bosch process for the production of artificial nitrogen fertilizers. Another famous example is 1920s Argentina. Briefly one of the "richest" countries in the world—on a par with France and Germany—in the 1930s Argentina experienced a collapse because of a dramatic decline in global demand for beef. A true high-income country, the kind of country that people in other countries aspire to emulate, is one that has a productive, stable, diversified economy that supports a high level of well-being for the broad majority of the population.

In real high-income countries, in the kinds of successful countries that others want to emulate, most people have high incomes (by global standards), even relatively poor people. Such countries are the exception in the world, not the rule. No more than thirty or forty countries (out of some two hundred) fall into this category, many of them quite small. They are nearly all concentrated in or near northwestern Europe or are descended from the settler colonies of the United Kingdom. Provocatively, nearly all of today's high-income countries were already the world's high-income countries in the 1810s. Two hundred years of economic growth have not overturned this basic hierarchy in the global economy, and although a few countries have caught up, none of the historically successful countries have fallen behind. It is an amazing fact that since the beginning of the Industrial Revolution not a single country has ever declined from high-income status to middle- or low-income status.

The robustness of high-income countries, the fact that they remain high-income countries through civil wars, world wars, political gridlock, political revolutions, financial crises, recessions, depressions, and recoveries, suggests that there is something more to it than just getting the policies right. Much more remarkable than the fact that so few middle-income countries have pursued sufficiently good policies to join the high-income club is the fact that not a single high-income country has pursued sufficiently bad policies to fall out of it. The so-called middle-income trap may not be a trap at all. It may be that the high-income countries are the ones trapped—pleasantly and fortuitously—in economic systems that perform well no matter what policies they pursue. The challenge for middle-income countries is to "fall up" into that same trap. Middle-income countries seem to experience high levels of economic mobility (just look at China and India) and high levels of policy responsiveness (viz Russia after communism, South Africa after apartheid). They can hardly be called trapped. Capped is more like it.

High income status is an all-pervasive quality of a country's economy, polity, and society. Clearly the BRICSs don't have it—yet. But all countries have the potential for positive social change, and the BRICSs have shown greater adaptability than most. What they lack most of all is appropriate guidance. No one policy reform will transform a middle-income country into a high-income country, just as no one policy failure (or even suite of failures) has been enough to transform a high-income country into a middle-income country. But a broad set of guidelines for large-scale economic, political, and social change can be assembled out of past experiences viewed through appropriate theoretical lenses. Get the governance right, get the demand side right, get the supply side right, and get the international linkages right, and the market will take care of the rest.

Obviously all of that is much easier said than done. But saying it is the first step. This book links the theory and practice of development economics to present a road map for escaping the middle-income trap. It starts from a thorough statistical analysis of the economic trajectories of the BRICS countries and proceeds by using these to illustrate what works and what might work for middle-income countries of all acronyms.

In the spirit of Heckman, our goal is to anticipate the effects of new (but well supported) policies in new (but well understood) environments with the ultimate goal of fostering broad-based economic growth. Chapter 1 summarizes and compares the economic, political, and social trajectories of the BRICS countries over the last twenty-five years. Chapter 2 focuses on the ways states have in the past and can still today mobilize economic rents to promote the development and growth of new industries. Chapter 3 picks up on the central role of the state in fostering mass demand for a country's products through policies that raise the incomes of ordinary workers. Chapter 4 demonstrates how middle-income countries can strategically position themselves in global markets in ways that generate the maximum learning and development for their own economies. The Conclusion argues that catch-up is possible but only if BRICS leaders put aside personal and parochial interests to pursue growth strategies that look beyond a narrow elite to benefit their entire populations.

1 THE BRICS TRAJECTORIES: ECONOMIC, POLITICAL, AND SOCIAL

The BRICS countries are neither leaders nor followers, neither rich nor poor, neither successful nor unsuccessful. They stand for the great in-between. Other large in-betweens include the MINTs (Mexico, Indonesia, Nigeria, Turkey) and also many non-acronym countries like Argentina, Colombia, Iran, Kazakhstan, Malaysia, and Thailand. All of eastern Europe might look much like the BRICSs were it not for the influence of European Union membership (or its promise). All of these countries have reasonably well functioning economies that participate in global value chains and support Western style consumerism, at least among a privileged portion of the population. All have the state capacity to manage their own affairs, though they often manage these affairs in short-sighted and morally dubious ways. All have societies that are recognizably modern in the central cities but notably less modern in more remote regions. And all of them seem prone to sometimes catastrophic environmental degradation, especially air, soil, and water pollution.

Brazil is by far the largest country of Latin America and in many ways representative of the region. In contrast to the rest of the region, Brazilians speak Portuguese, not Spanish, but otherwise Brazil's culture, religion, and historical experiences parallel those of its neighbors very closely. Brazil achieved its independence from Portugal in the 1820s, at the same time as Spain's American colonies. Like most of Latin America, Brazil is a predominantly Catholic country populated by the descendants of a mix of (mostly southern) European colonizers, indigenous Americans, and African slaves. Brazil makes up about 40 percent of the total population of Latin America and is only slightly richer than average for the region. Like many other countries in the region, it has experienced wild political swings between left-wing populist governments and ultraconservative military dictatorships. Also like most of the region, its violent internal politics have been matched by remarkably peaceful external relations. Brazil is again typical for its high levels of criminality and inequality paired with traditional Catholic family values. In short, Brazil is important as Brazil, but it is just as important as a stand-in for Latin America as a whole.

Russia has a very different history and is perhaps the most distinctive of the BRICSs. Before 1917 Russia might have been considered representative of eastern Europe in the same way as Brazil is representative of Latin America: larger and a little richer than its peers, but similar in culture and social structure. But the events of the last one hundred years changed all that. Soviet communism, experienced as an indigenous development inside Russia, was experienced as an external force in the rest of the Soviet Union and eastern Europe. Since the 1990s most of Russia's former client states have linked their economies to that of the European Union, leaving Russia (along with Ukraine, Belarus, and a motley collection of other jurisdictions) out in the cold. Thus although Russia is in itself an important country—a nuclear superpower, the world's largest country by area, the ninth largest by population, by most counts a top-ten economy, and a collection of similar superlatives—it is not very representative of other middle-income countries. Poland might be a better proxy for postcommunist Europe. But Russia is permanently fixed on the global agenda in a way that Poland is not.

India is the dominant country of South Asia, constituting more than 70 percent of the population and economy of the region. Nearly all of South Asia was part of the British Empire until partition and independence in 1947, as were substantial portions of Southeast Asia. Strong Indian cultural influences extend as far east as Bali in Indonesia, and British Indian historical influence extended as far west as present-day Iraq. Although all of the countries in the region are distinctive and many of them are bitter rivals, India is nonetheless a useful proxy for understanding the economic pressures and opportunities experienced by all of the countries in the broad region running from Iran to Indonesia. India itself, with a population of 1.25 billion, is home to more people than the entire continent of Africa and is an important country in its own right. India's northern state of Uttar Pradesh, with a population of around 200 million, is much larger (and much poorer) than Nigeria, while other areas of India are home to world-class software and business process outsourcing industries. India's sheer size and diversity make it a useful country for international comparisons.

China is, of course, China. No discussion of emerging market economies, their successes, the challenges they face, and their aspirations for the future would make sense without China. China is the most populous country in the world, the second in land area, and the second-largest economy. It is first in international trade. More importantly, it has risen from being one of the ten poorest countries in the world at the beginning of its reform period in 1978 to being firmly in the middle of the world's income distribution today. This miracle is not really as miraculous as it seems: China in 1978 had many of the social and political attributes of a middle-income country, even if its measured economic output was very small in dollar terms. That said, there is no denying the appeal of China's story—nor the reality of the transformation that underlies it. Where the other BRICSs tell stories of rise and fall, China tells a story of rise and rise. Where the other BRICSs offer promise for the future, China offers promise for the present. People in developing countries rarely talk about emulating Brazil, Russia, India, or South Africa. They talk about becoming the next China.

South Africa is a latecomer to the BRICSs, not one of the acronym creator Jim O'Neill's original BRICs but a later addition. South Africa got itself added to the BRICs through a decade-long political lobbying effort; it is perhaps the only country to ever successfully lobby to join an acronym. But though it may seem strange to people outside the investment community, lobbying to be included in multinational stock market indices and emerging-market asset managers' international allocation lists is actually quite routine. Hundreds of billions of dollars of portfolio investment are benchmarked to these indices and lists. South Africa's inclusion in the BRICSs gives it greater access to international capital markets and the opportunity to exercise influence in emerging BRICS institutions like the Shanghai-based New Development Bank. South Africa's inclusion is analytically meaningful as well. South Africa is the leading economy of sub-Saharan Africa and a realistic example for the rest of Africa to follow. It shares in many of the social and health challenges of the region but is nonetheless a (relatively) stable democracy with a middle-income economy. While it may be difficult to imagine a path from the Congo basin to the Pearl River Delta, it seems easier to imagine a path to the Cape of Good Hope.

The five BRICS countries are all very different, yet somehow, too, they are the same. Somehow the label sticks, and not just because it makes for an easy-to-pronounce acronym. The "MINTs" sounds just as clever but has failed to capture the popular imagination. These countries also represent a wide range of human experience, but they lack the sense of commonality conjured up by the BRICSs. The BRICS countries may come from very different backgrounds, but they seem to be ending up in a similar place. They all have or are approaching middle-income status, to be sure. But they also share high levels of state capacity coupled with extraordinarily high levels of income inequality. They all have functioning education and health systems even if there are serious inequities in access to services. Students actually want to study at BRICS universities, which is (much) more than can be said for universities in most of the developing world. The BRICS political systems run the gamut from wildly democratic to oppressively authoritarian, but whatever their levels of democracy all of them are characterized by winner-take-all politics and a high level of central control. Like most of the rest of the developing world, all five BRICS countries have questionable records when it comes to environmental governance.

Perhaps most importantly, the BRICS countries have flatly refused to play by the set of rules laid out by Western governments and intergovernmental organizations in the "Washington Consensus" model of development. The 1990s Washington Consensus stressed liberalization (of trade, investment, interest rates, and exchange rates), privatization, deregulation, the elimination of subsidies, and the protection of property rights. The BRICSs (and especially China) have flagrantly violated all of these principles. Yet they (and especially China) are perceived to have succeeded where others have failed. This success is to some degree real and to some degree illusory, but that it has been accomplished in defiance of advice from Washington is certainly true. The BRICSs have stuck a finger (or five) in the eye of the Washington Consensus, and Washington itself, and for that they are widely admired through-out the developing world (and beyond). Whether or not they will continue to be admired in five, ten, or twenty years' time depends on what they make of the successes they have enjoyed so far.

THE BRICS ECONOMIES

The BRICS mystique arose first in the economic sphere, and it is in the economic sphere that they are perceived to have scored their greatest successes. In 2011 Jim O'Neill identified the BRICs (minus South Africa) as the emerging market economies to watch, and in fact between 2000 and 2015 the BRICSs were some of the best-performing economies in the world. In the first fifteen years of the twenty-first century, the world's developed economies experienced the bursting of the dot-com bubble in 2000–2001, the global financial crisis of 2008–9, and the ongoing euro crisis that began in 2010. Over that period the developed world's best-performing major economy, the United States, experienced real (inflation adjusted) annual gross domestic product (GDP) growth of less than 2 percent per year. Major European and Asian economies fared worse. By contrast every one of the BRICS economies exceeded 3 percent annual growth, with Russia recording 4.5 percent, India 7 percent, and China nearly 10 percent compound annual growth in real GDP. The economies of Brazil and South Africa were some 50 percent larger in 2015 than they were in 2010. Russia's economy was nearly twice the size and India's nearly three times. China's economy quadrupled in size, rising to the second largest in the world.

The economic growth of the BRICS countries—even that of the weaker BRICS economies of Brazil and South Africa—was truly impressive in the first years of the new millennium. But a wider perspective offers different insights. Figure 1 charts the long-term economic trajectories of the five BRICS countries since 1980. Each line represents a country's GDP per capita expressed as a percentage of the US level for the same year. For this comparison the BRICS countries' GDPs have been converted into US dollars using standard purchasing power parity (PPP) conversion rates, which smooth out the annual volatility that can make comparisons difficult when using market exchange rates. The longer thirty-five-year view presented in the figure leaves a very different impression from the recent fifteen-year timeframe over which the BRICS economies are usually judged.

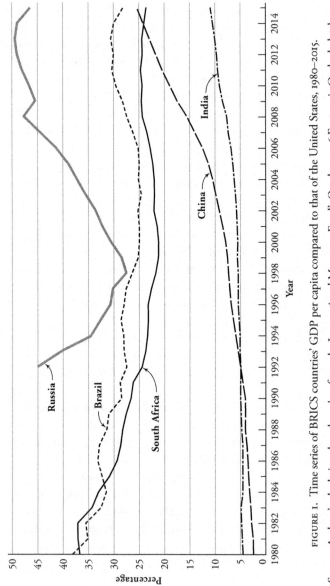

FIGURE 1. Time series of BRICS countries' GDP per capita compared to that of the United States, 1980–2015.

Source: Authors' calculations based on data from the International Monetary Fund's October 2016 Economic Outlook database.

A few facts are obvious from even a quick glance at Figure 1. First, Brazil and South Africa haven't done very well at all when viewed over a longer time frame. In fact, they've been bouncing up and down between 20 and 40 percent of US levels of GDP per capita for as long as such data have existed. The perennial "sleeping giant" of Latin America, Brazil in particular has repeatedly been named as a potential challenger to the United States for regional economic supremacy, most recently in the 1970s—just before entering twenty years of relative stagnation. South Africa's economy declined dramatically throughout the late apartheid era and only began to recover several years after its transition to full democracy in 1994.

Second, Russia's dramatic growth in the first decade of the new century was nothing more than a bounce back from Russia's equally dramatic decline in the last decade of the old century. The economic merits of communism may be difficult to judge using contemporary economic measures like GDP per capita, but there is no doubt that Russia's transition from communism to capitalism was accompanied by massive economic dislocation. Whether or not the "shock therapy" (as it has come to be called) of the early 1990s was a necessary or appropriate policy for Russia can be and has been debated, but there can be little doubt that Russia's high rate of economic growth after 1999 is due at least in part to a bounce back to Russia's previously established levels of output. Between 1992 and 1998 Russia's labor force participation rate fell from 70 percent to 61 percent, suggesting a sharp drop in capacity utilization. Since 1998 it has returned to 69 percent, the highest in the BRICSs and much higher than in the United States. The collapse of communism was a supply-side shock from which Russia had only just recovered when it ran into Western economic sanctions stemming from the Ukraine crisis in 2014.

Third, India and China are the only two of the five BRICS countries that exhibit secular growth paths spanning the last quarter century. Both started their current trajectories following major reforms that opened their economies to the outside world. The Communist Party of China officially heralded the beginning of the reform era in its historic December 22, 1978, communiqué, in which it exhorted the Chinese people to "advance courageously to make a fundamental change in the backward state of our country." The rest is history. Careful historians point out the social foundations for growth laid down during the collectivist era of Mao Zedong and the precursors of reform in China leading up to 1978. But the post-1978 growth in China has been epic. India, by contrast, had a much less extreme break with the past following a 1991 foreign exchange crisis. In the 1990s India liberalized its currency, dismantled its system of import licensing, and eliminated many government monopolies, especially monopolies for the sale of imported goods. There was also widespread industrial deregulation. As in China a decade earlier, growth in India accelerated as India began to converge toward middle-income status.

And that's the point. Absent self-destructive policies that isolated their economies from the larger global economy, China has converged and India is converging toward middle-income status. Neither country has experienced so much as a single year of negative growth since the beginning of its reform and opening process. Their direction has been uniformly upward—toward the middle. Brazil and South Africa, having long been in the middle, wobble up and down with no clear direction in sight. Russia, the only one of the BRICSs that is also a major energy exporter, has seen its economic fortunes rise and fall with the global oil price. Oil and gas account for more than two-thirds of Russia's exports and as much as a quarter of the entire Russian economy. The 2014 collapse in oil prices cost the Russian economy dearly—or one might just as well argue that the ninefold increase in oil prices between 1999 and 2011 benefited the Russian economy mightily. If China and India are best understood as middle-income countries in the making, Russia might be best understood as a middle-income country plus oil. All three are joining a club that Brazil and South Africa have exemplified for decades.

A careful look at Figure 1 reveals that the five BRICS countries are all converging in GDP per capita relative to the United States. Despite very different starting points (both economic and historical) they are converging toward income levels that are roughly one-quarter that of the United States. China may yet grow past this point, but its growth began to slow decisively in 2015 and even the Chinese government has now embraced the rhetoric of a "new normal" era of slower growth. With the exception of Russia's unique post-1991 experience, Figure 1 doesn't give any suggestion of historical instability that might presage an impending collapse. But it does suggest that there's not much to the BRICS story after all. Viewed in isolation China's rise has been extraordinary. Viewed in comparative perspective, China has "merely" joined the long-standing middle-income club. China's rise may have been extraordinary in its scale and speed, but it has brought China to an all too ordinary destination. Whereas India has been slow to rise to economic mediocrity, China has been very fast.

Looking beyond the BRICSs, the entire middle-income tier of the global economy (which includes much of Latin America, the Middle East, east-central Europe, and South Asia) recapitulates the general pattern of long-term rise and fall within the broad band of 15–35 percent of US GDP per capita. Over the long term the US economy has grown on average around 2 percent per year, and over the last century or more the middle-income band has grown along with it, benefiting from technological improvements and foreign investment that originate in the United States and other developed countries. But the basic structural relationship between the economies of the United States (the world's leading economy and leading foreign investor since before World War I) and the middle-income band has remained remarkably stable over the long term. For example, the overall GDP per capita of Latin America as a whole has fluctuated within the narrow band of 20–29 percent of the US level of GDP per capita for the entire century since 1913. The equivalent range for east-central Europe is 19–33 percent and for the Middle East, 18–34 percent. The middle-income regions of the world have been stably middle income for a very long time.

The BRICS economies may be similar in GDP per capita, but in other aspects they have taken many different economic paths to arrive at similar income levels. For example Brazil has a very large service sector (71% of GDP, similar to European levels) while China's economy is built around massive levels of investment (44% of GDP, among the highest in the world). Brazil has very high levels of government debt (65% of GDP) while Russia has very low levels (18%). India and South Africa still have very large agricultural sectors (both 18% of GDP) while Brazil and Russia no longer do (6% and 4%). Brazil is a major agricultural exporter even though agriculture accounts for a relatively small portion of Brazil's total economy. Brazil, India, and South Africa routinely run large trade deficits; China and Russia run large surpluses. All figures here are for 2014, but these general patterns are relatively stable. There is no such thing as a BRICS economy, except that all of the BRICS economies generate levels of GDP per capita that place them roughly in the middle of the global income distribution.

There are, however, two characteristics that all of the BRICSs share in common. They all have extraordinarily high levels of inequality, and they all leak capital like a sieve. In these two qualities the BRICSs lead the world.

Despite their middle-income status, the four original BRIC countries are all on the *Hurun Report*'s top-ten list of countries with the most billionaires. The one BRICS country not on the list, South Africa, is itself by most measures the most unequal country in the world, with a Gini coefficient of 60 or more. The Gini coefficient is a measure of inequality that runs from a low of 0 (all income is shared equally) to a high of 100 (all income is concentrated in one person's hands). Inequality is notoriously difficult to measure and strictly comparable international data are not available, but South Africa seems to be about as bad as it gets.

Until recently Brazil was just as unequal as South Africa, but Brazil's Gini coefficient seems to have declined to the low 50s in recent years. Meanwhile China's has risen to the low 50s (no one knows for sure) and Russia reports an unrealistically low Gini coefficient in the low 40s. For comparison, the United States has a disposable income Gini coefficient of around 40 and most European countries are in the low 30s. Of the five BRICS countries only India seems to have relatively low levels of measured income inequality (a Gini of around 34) due to the fact that so few people in India have any money at all. The gap between rich and poor is wider in India than in any of the other BRICS countries, but there are so few rich people that they hardly show up in the statistics.

All five BRICSs are also among the top seven sources of illicit financial flows, according to the American NGO Global Financial Integrity. Rounding out the top seven are Mexico and Malaysia. Another term for "illicit financial flows" is capital flight. The BRICS economies are plagued by high levels of capital flight in part because they do generate large fortunes and in part because they do not generate sufficient opportunities for those fortunes to be put to work at home rather than abroad. As the *Hurun Report* and *Forbes* magazine "rich list" biographies demonstrate, many BRICS billionaires make their money in sectors that are closely linked to government and thus highly reliant on political favor. The BRICS fortunes are apt to be built on rents (money made by exploiting politically created market imperfections) rather than profits (returns to capital in a well-functioning market). Having accumulated large fortunes by collecting rents, BRICS billionaires then look for profitable investment opportunities overseas. The essence of capitalism is the reinvestment of profits to generate yet more capital, but rents do not generate additional rents. In the BRICS countries as in other developing countries, it is often easier to extract value than to create value. And the extraction of value is not an economic activity but a political one.

THE BRICS GOVERNMENTS

It almost goes without saying that the BRICS countries are staggeringly corrupt. In 2016 Brazil's president Dilma Rousseff was impeached in connection with a corruption scandal involving the state oil company, Petrobras. The opposition president of Brazil's Chamber of Deputies—the person who led the impeachment effort against Rousseff—was himself removed from office due to corruption charges related to Petrobras. Meanwhile the secret wealth controlled by Russia's president Vladimir Putin has reportedly been assessed at $40 billion by the CIA (in 2007). No one knows the accuracy of this claim, but the scale of Russian corruption was underscored during Russia's hosting of the 2014 Winter Olympics, which cost even more than Beijing's extravagant 2008 Summer Olympic games. In India scandals involving government telecommunications licensing and coal contracts in 2010 and 2012 cost the government a combined $73 billion. India's 2010 hosting of the Commonwealth Games ran some seventeen times over budget, like the Sochi Olympics a record widely attributed to corruption. The Chinese government itself acknowledges that the Chinese government is highly corrupt. In 2012 it estimated that some 18,000 corrupt officials had fled the country since the opening of the reform era, and instituted an anticorruption campaign that has since "disciplined" more than 750,000 government officials. In South Africa the president, Jacob Zuma, has faced repeated corruption investigations (but no convictions) throughout his political career. The government of South Africa disbanded its "Scorpions" anticorruption investigation unit in 2009.

The amazing thing about all of this is that the BRICS countries are not considered especially corrupt by international standards. The Western-government and corporate-funded NGO Transparency International ranks Russia 131st out of 176 countries for the cleanliness of its government, with Brazil, India, and China tied for 79th and South Africa performing the best of the BRICSs at 64th, on its

2016 Corruption Perceptions Index. Those performances put all except Russia in the top half of all rated countries. America's NAFTA partner Mexico comes in at number 95, worse than all the BRICSs except Russia. South Africa is even tied with Italy, a founding member of the G7 and the European Union. Though the endemic political corruption of the BRICS countries may shock Western observers and outrage their own citizens, it is merely representative of the human experience. If the scale of BRICS corruption is shockingly large, it is simply because the BRICSs are themselves relatively large countries, not because the BRICSs are especially corrupt countries. The (scant) available evidence suggests that they are not.

Quite the contrary, the BRICS governments appear to function relatively well by contemporary international developing country standards. The BRICS countries are able to maintain national health and education systems, patrol their borders, collect taxes, pay public sector employees, and so on. All things considered, the BRICS states have the capacity to get things done when and where the political will exists to do so. They have also established their capacity for social control, whether through traditional means like policing and press censorship or through emerging means like online surveillance and antiterrorism operations. The ability of the BRICS states both to get things done and to prevent things getting done makes them gatekeepers in charge of access to some of the world's largest economies. Developed countries have similar (indeed, much greater) state capacities, but have ethical rules (backed up by strong institutional safeguards) against direct state intervention in the economy. The BRICS countries seem to have no such qualms.

A defining characteristic of the BRICS economies is the extent to which they are owned and managed by the state. Poorer developing countries also have high nominal levels of state involvement in the economy, but these countries often lack the capacity to turn state ownership into true state management. Thus although countries as diverse as Ecuador, Indonesia, and Nigeria have state oil companies, they lack the state capacity to exploit their oil resources without international help. By contrast, Brazil, Russia, and China all have technologically capable state oil companies that only need international assistance to solve the most challenging production problems. Thus although the heavy hand of the state can be found everywhere in the developing world (as reflected in Transparency International's corruption perceptions surveys), it is most effective in large, middle-income countries like the BRICSs. As a result, state connections are routinely required for doing business, and politics becomes in large part a battle for control of the state and its largesse. The private sector, as such, is underdeveloped and lacks autonomy. Even the private is political.

In short, although three of the BRICSs have vibrant electoral democracies (Brazil, India, South Africa), one has an autocratic managed democracy (Russia), and one has no elections and little accountability at the national level (China), all five are similar when it comes to the character of the state as experienced by businesses, consumers, and investors. Businesses of all kinds and at all levels must regularly make irregular payments to government (and/or party) officials in the ordinary course of doing business; bribery is endemic, not exceptional. Consumers have widespread normative expectations that the state will actively intervene to manage the prices of essential goods like housing, energy, and food—and in the case of housing, to make sure that resale values consistently rise over time. And investors take it for granted that the success or failure of any given investment project will depend in large part on maintaining government support—and may even require a government license to happen at all. In other words, all economic actors, from the poorest to the richest, are engaged one way or another, voluntarily or involuntarily, in the pursuit of political rents. Rent seeking, efforts to preserve existing rents, and the avoidance of rent payment are ordinary political activities in the BRICS economies. Any analysis of the middle-income trap must take such behaviors into account.

THE BRICS SOCIETIES

If the BRICS governments are distinguished by their capacity to facilitate economic rent seeking, their state capacity also allows them to accomplish broad social goals that are beyond the reach of many developing countries. Russia and China under communism transformed themselves from backward semifeudal societies into countries where women were empowered to participate in social and economic (if not political) life outside the household, where basic health and healthcare came to be taken for granted, and where nearly everyone would read and write. They also established sufficient scientific capacity to independently build nuclear power plants and nuclear bombs, space programs, and intercontinental ballistic missiles. If Russian (Soviet) development was far ahead of China's, it was at least in part because communist Russia started out much richer and more developed than communist China. Postcommunist Russia experienced a wrenching transition to capitalism in the 1990s—an experience for the most part avoided in China (so far)—but contemporary Russia and contemporary China continue to demonstrate the capacity to execute megaprojects like Russia's new Vostochny space center and China's expanding high-speed rail network. Whatever the merits of the goals these two countries set out to achieve under communism and beyond, their states have clearly demonstrated the capacity to mobilize their societies to pursue them.

The more democratic BRICSs of Brazil, India, and South Africa have stronger records of social development. Brazil's flagship social welfare program, the Bolsa Familia, launched in 2003, was almost scuppered in 2005 by media reports of widespread benefits fraud. This is when the Brazilian state showed its capacity to implement and enforce: instead of canceling the program as critics demanded, the government successfully mobilized resources to monitor and audit the disbursement of Bolsa Familia benefits.

The program is widely reputed to be well run and effective; it is held up by international NGOs and intergovernmental institutions like the World Bank as an example to be emulated throughout the developing world.

Less well publicized has been the success of South Africa's housing and social grants programs. South Africa's successes may not have achieved the same level of notoriety as Brazil's, but their record is similar: seventeen million people served by direct cash transfers, successful targeting of the poorest households, and relatively low levels of waste and misappropriation. Perhaps because South Africa's programs are unconditional—and thus out of step with contemporary neoliberal policy prescriptions—they have not been widely promoted by international NGOs and intergovernmental institutions as models for the rest of the developing world. Nonetheless, they demonstrate the administrative capacity of a state that is often pilloried in the international press for the extravagantly politically incorrect public pronouncements of its leaders. The sharp contrast between leadership failure and administrative success in South Africa is illustrated by the country's response to the AIDS crisis. Under the administration of Thabo Mbeki (1999–2008) the South African health services were actively prevented from responding appropriately to the AIDS epidemic, with disastrous consequences for public health. When his immediate successor, Kgalema Motlanthe (2008–9), reversed his policies, South Africa's health services were able to make rapid gains in controlling the disease. Even though the next president, Jacob Zuma, repeatedly made embarrassing public comments regarding AIDS, the state public health institutions continue to function effectively.

India is much poorer than the other BRICSs and has correspondingly lower levels of state capacity. Social welfare programs in India are correspondingly underdeveloped and poorly managed. India may have nuclear weapons and a space program, but it seems unable to administer even a straightforward food distribution scheme without serious problems of misallocation and corruption. Twenty-first-century India is still struggling with malnutrition, lack of sanitation, uncontrolled infectious disease, and (in some places) severe gender inequalities culminating in female infanticide, widespread rape, and bride trafficking. Unlike the other BRICSs, where extreme poverty is disappearing, India remains one of the world's largest reservoirs of poor subsistence farmers. In some ways India can be thought of as two countries in one: nuclear-armed India and machete-wielding India. Nuclear India is socially comparable to the other BRICS countries; village India is not.

India does however seem to be making steady progress in overall social indicators like education and life expectancy. Average years of schooling have more than doubled since 1980 to nearly seven years, though this is still below the levels of Brazil (eight years), Russia (twelve years), China (eight years), and South Africa (ten years). Life expectancy is steadily improving. Figure 2 charts the evolution of life expectancy at birth of the five BRICS countries since 1980. Each line represents a country's life expectancy (in years) expressed as a percentage of American life expectancy for the same year. Overall life expectancy is considered a broad, all-encompassing indicator of societal strength because so many different aspects of society combine to affect mortality at different age levels: maternal care, child nutrition, vaccination, education, road safety, mosquito control, sanitation infrastructure, smoking policies, and of course hospital care. Figure 2 shows that China and Brazil have consistently rising life expectancy approaching US levels, that Russia is slowly returning to levels of life expectancy it enjoyed before its postcommunist transition, that South Africa's rising trajectory was tragically interrupted by its mishandling of the AIDS epidemic, and that India is twenty years behind Brazil but consistently improving. Even if the BRICS countries are seemingly stuck at one-third of US income levels, their equilibrium level of life expectancy may be 95

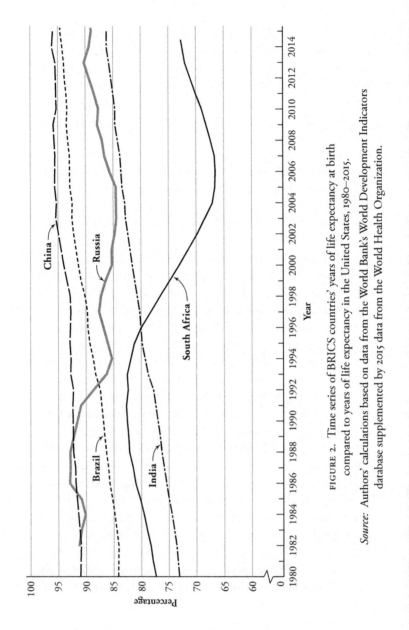

FIGURE 2. Time series of BRICS countries' years of life expectancy at birth compared to years of life expectancy in the United States, 1980–2015.

Source: Authors' calculations based on data from the World Bank's World Development Indicators database supplemented by 2015 data from the World Health Organization.

percent of that of the United States. This suggests that the middle-income trap may not be very bad for your health, even if it is indisputably bad for your wallet.

The main social challenge in the BRICS countries (and in middle-income countries more generally) may not be the failure of the state to deliver social services but the failure of society itself to coalesce into a meaningful whole. Each of the BRICSs has its own historical legacy that may account for the failure of civil society—slavery in Brazil, communism in Russia and China, colonialism in India, apartheid in South Africa—but the surplus of legacies in the BRICSs and other middle-income countries suggests that something deeper and more structural may be at work. Like all late developers, the BRICS countries have grown up in a world in which rich countries already exist. This may have affected their societies more than their economies. In many ways Brazilian society is focused on Miami and New York; Russian, Indian, and South African society on London; Chinese civil society on Hong Kong and California. Elite BRICS students aren't educated in their home countries; they go to universities (and make lifelong connections) in the United States and United Kingdom. The life chances of BRICS elites are divorced from the realities of the BRICS societies in a way that was not possible for American and European elites during the formation of their own countries' modern civil societies.

The fact that the fates of BRICS elites are disconnected from the fates of their compatriots may have little impact on bread-and-butter economic variables like investment, consumption, and interest rates, but it is likely to have a big impact on the formulation of economic policy. All elites may be predisposed to favor policies that favor themselves, but this is perhaps not so much a problem when the interests of elites are broadly aligned with those of society as a whole. The character of the economic policies adopted by the state may be especially important in BRICS countries due to the outsized role of the state in the economy. Even the most effective state institutions can only be effective at achieving the goals that they are actually assigned to accomplish. If those goals represent elite interests that clash with broader societal interests, then strong states may impede rather than promote the development of the economy as a whole. Ultimately it may be the BRICS societies, more than their economies, that are stuck in a middle-income trap.

2 THE ROLE OF THE STATE IN ECONOMIC DEVELOPMENT

The rise of the BRICSs has occurred during a period in which the idea that the state should act as a motor for economic development has been largely discredited. A wide variety of forms of state involvement in the economy emerged in the twentieth century, from the communist revolutions in Russia and China to the peasant wars in postcolonial states to the liberal welfare states of Europe and North America. Throughout the developing world, state involvement in the economy was particularly strong, partly following the lead of the more developed countries and partly because local economic elites were weak and lacked entrepreneurial experience. Dire social needs often took precedence over economics, and state-owned (and newly nationalized) companies were routinely used to provide welfare services for their workers and the community at large.

Many of these attempts at state-guided development failed when the world debt crisis of the 1980s broke out. The state-led developing economies of the 1960s and 1970s were largely based on import-substitution industrialization: import restrictions forced consumers to buy domestically manufactured products, effectively levying a tax on the entire consumer population. Governments also extracted high levels of rents from commodity export goods like minerals and agricultural products. Both import substitution and rent extraction tend to dampen technological advancement because they eliminate incentives to innovate. As a result, governments had to pour more and more capital into inefficient industries just to keep production going. As production stagnated, so did consumption for the impoverished masses.

Ruling elites all across the developing world created the basis for private enrichment and concentrated power in the form of their control of the state economic machinery. This was true in nominally capitalist and communist countries alike. These ruling elites became the "state classes" that captured disproportionate shares of the benefits of their highly protected, highly centralized national economies. The state classes of the developing world promised that decolonization would bring about economic development, but what little success they had relied on massive quantities of borrowed capital. Economically unable to increase the efficiency of their bloated state industries and politically unable to let in foreign investment, the state classes borrowed to make ends meet.

That credit bubble burst in the early 1980s when the US Federal Reserve under the chairmanship of Paul Volcker suddenly raised interest rates to previously unheard-of levels in 1979–81. Unable to raise capital in New York and London, the leaders of developing countries could no longer sustain the economic subsidies that had been keeping their economies afloat. Brazil and India were among the countries worst affected. The South African economy stagnated. Even Russia was affected. Among the BRICSs only China, with no modern industry to speak of and no foreign debt, emerged unscathed.

However, it soon became obvious that some countries rode out the crisis much better than others, particularly the developing countries of East Asia. These countries slowly opened their economies to the outside world by increasing exports, gradually admitting foreign investment, adopting foreign technologies, declaring their philosophical adherence to free markets, and perhaps most importantly specializing according to comparative advantage. These newly industrializing countries, especially the four Asian tigers of Hong Kong, Singapore, South Korea, and Taiwan, could be thought of as special cases for a variety of reasons. But they succeeded.

Many books have been written about the four Asian tigers, offering many theories about the reasons for their success; but one way or another they all created competitive economies with profit incentives for productive investment. All authors agree that they did not do this by freeing up the magic of the market, as mainstream economics might teach. Capitalism with a profit mechanism and perfect competition is not a natural state of an economy. Under conditions of underdevelopment it requires strong government intervention to create high incentives for productive investment. Ignoring mainstream economic advice, this is precisely what the four tigers did.

The proper state regulation of the market requires mechanisms through which the final demand for goods and services is increased. Ultimately this demand must come from the consumption of goods and services by the working class, but in the short term it can come from accelerated investment, increasing middle-class consumption, and surpluses in foreign trade. In other words, states must ensure that it is profitable for people to invest in their economies by making sure that there is always a ready market for increased production. And they have to do this in a way that prevents the emergence of the kinds of concentrated economic and political power that can choke off productive investment through rent-seeking behavior. Market competition is the best mechanism yet developed for dispersing power and thus forcing people to innovate if they want to make money.

Accomplishing this balancing act requires specific kinds of power relations within society, which first came into existence in northwestern Europe and later spread throughout what is now the developed world of the West. Mainstream economists working in the traditions of endogenous growth theory and neoinstitutional theory agree that in order to get the economy right it is first necessary to get the society right, and the countries that first got the society right are mainly those of northwestern European heritage. But there the consensus ends. What is it about northwestern European societies that makes them the "right" kinds for supporting high-productivity modern economies? It is difficult to answer that question without ideological blinders.

We take a comparative approach, leaving aside the ideology to focus on results. After World War II first Japan and then the four Asian tigers created mass markets through high wages for urban workers and (except in Hong Kong and Singapore) land redistribution for rural farmers. All five countries spurred exports by keeping their currencies undervalued. With the exception of Hong Kong, they attracted foreign investment by letting their currencies appreciate over time. Though Japan and (to some extent) South Korea are famous for their economic planning, Japan and the four tigers all relied on market mechanisms for the allocation of capital. Scholars may debate the larger social and political forces that allowed these countries to pursue mass consumption policies within a market economy framework, but the fact that they did is what interests us—and what accounts for their rapid development in the second half of the twentieth century.

The BRICSs share none of these features. Instead the BRICSs exhibit many of the characteristics that were common in developing countries in the middle of the twentieth century. They generate large economic surpluses in their state-controlled and resource-extraction sectors, in industries like telecommunications and oil, but these surpluses tend to be captured by the powerful economic and political elites of the state class. Mobilizing these surpluses for productive investment requires support from the (highly politicized and inevitably corrupt) nonmarket sphere. This is theoretically possible but empirically unprecedented.

Yet the BRICSs are not just unreconstructed 1970s third world economies. To begin with, they are now all much more integrated into the larger global economy than they were forty years ago, and they all have more or less free exchange rates. Brazil has gone through multiple structural adjustment programs and has a much smaller state sector than it once did. Russia of course has a completely different economic system from the one it had under the Soviet Union. India dumped the "license Raj" in the 1990s and now has a dynamic services export sector. China has become a hybrid economy with closely controlled large enterprises (whether private or state owned) supplemented by a fiercely competitive small- and medium-enterprise sector. South Africa saw a dramatic rise in the power of organized labor with the transition from apartheid to majority rule. Today's BRICSs are neither old-style third world economies nor newly industrialized tiger economies—and they are certainly not liberal Western economies. They do not fit neatly into the typical categories of mainstream economic debates about the opposition between market economics and central management. They are stuck somewhere between dirigisme and development.

THE GENERATION OF RENTS

From the outset of developmentalism, the interaction between state regulation and market forces has been fine-tuned at the political level. In the world of the 1950s, with the example of the Soviet Union's centrally managed economy (which resisted the world economic crisis of the 1930s much better than the capitalist West and was able to defeat industrialized Germany in World War II), central planning appeared manageable and promising to the countries of the Global South. Postcolonial elites were able to massively increase the share of investment in total product compared to the levels of investment that had prevailed under colonial rule, since colonial administrations had had little incentive to develop the countries they ruled. Colonial administrations had instead used the surplus generated by society to maintain themselves and their colonial clients, tolerating large precapitalist economies and depressing the purchasing power of the people they ruled.

The investments of the postcolonial developmental states could not be immediately profitable because of the distortions in the economic structures of underdeveloped economies (principally a lack of mass demand). They were thus protected from competition. The leaders of the investment class were incentivized to play political power games rather than pursue technical innovation. In order to repress such political games more market mechanisms were required, and these were demanded by international institutions like the World Bank and the International Monetary Fund in exchange for loans and support. As a result, the management of the available surplus was increasingly oriented to market signals as economies shifted to neoliberal reforms, a process known as rationalization.

The simultaneous existence of surpluses and a weakness of capitalist mechanisms for absorbing them into immediately profitable investment explains the limited degree of market regulation in most underdeveloped economies. That part of the surplus generated by an economy that cannot be appropriated by the market without some degree of market imperfection (be it in monopolies, entrapped contracts, or state guarantees) can be defined as rent. Underdeveloped economies are characterized by the simultaneous existence of rents and profits. If private capitalists cannot appropriate rents without using them in ways that are economically inefficient, the state must step in. When private capitalists are able to reinvest rents productively, it may be unfair in relation to competitors but it does not harm the economy. When private capitalists are incentivized to use rents unproductively, they must be prevented from acquiring them in the first place.

The coexistence of both profits and rents in underdeveloped economies does not constitute a particular variety of capitalism. It is instead a characteristic of an essentially noncapitalist economy, because the existence of rents implies that the access to economic surpluses depends primarily on nonmarket mechanisms. In such environments profit-based capitalism is too weak to cohere the whole society and has not only to tolerate but even to require the vitality of a noncapitalist sector. The more the noncapitalist sector is free from having to follow the criterion of maximizing its own profit, the freer it is to subsidize and enable the capitalist sector. The capitalist sector may and will remove this sector when the problem of overcoming underdevelopment and the establishment of full-fledged capitalism is made possible. With booming demand, capitalist entrepreneurs are able to build strong enough coalitions for imposing a functioning capitalist system against the existing noncapitalist structures.

In seeking to clarify the logic of the interaction between capitalist and noncapitalist sectors, parenthetical definitions of capitalism (like varieties of capitalism) are not very useful. Such concepts conceal the real issue: systems which incorporate a large rent-generating sector can still develop productively by using those rents in the interest of development. In order to overcome underdevelopment and eliminate rent structures at the same time, countries have to mobilize rents for the establishment of a capitalist structure upon which profits can flourish because demand is expanding. And practically speaking that expanding demand has to come from meeting the needs and desires of the broad mass of the population. In countries where the vast majority of the population is very poor, mass demand has to come from the poor, and to make that possible the incomes of the poor must be raised to the point where they can become mass consumers.

SUPPORTING THE PRIVATE SECTOR

The precise shape of the relation between the capitalist and the non-capitalist sector is largely determined by the historical trajectory of the respective societies, and the BRICS countries have very different systems of state involvement in the economy. The five countries place different degrees of importance on transnational enterprises, especially in their foreign trade sector, and have different mechanisms for "guiding" the national and international private sectors through market regulation. But levels of government spending as a percentage of GDP are similar (ranging from a low of 27% in India to a high of 39% in Brazil), and the BRICSs share with advanced capitalist economies a sense of government responsibility for public goods, long-term growth, and the regulation of the monetary sectors of the economy. They also all have sophisticated monetary systems that serve to regulate the different sectors of the economy and the relation of their economies with the outside world.

The BRICS countries have also all made provisions for mobilizing rents to help them overcome underdevelopment. Public goods (like education, transportation, and financial infrastructures) are crucial for the proper functioning of capitalist economies. The BRICSs have inherited infrastructures of different quality, but they have all decided to invest in road building, power distribution, ports, and administrative and educational infrastructures. China has invested incredible amounts in transportation infrastructure, building by far the world's largest high-speed railway system (more than 20,000 km, with plans to increase to 30,000 km by 2020) and the world's biggest highway system (85,000 km, versus 76,000 for the United States). Russia, with extensive infrastructure inherited from the Soviet Union, has been much less spectacular in this domain, while India and South Africa lag despite ambitious plans. China, Russia, and Brazil have energy transportation systems which allow industry to be supplied without serious interruptions, while India has scheduled renovation of energy transportation systems as a major target and South Africa suffers serious power shortages.

Investment in education, particularly higher education, is constrained by a bias toward spending on items that show a more immediate return. It is easier to justify investments in physical infrastructure (like a tunnel or bridge) than investments in human infrastructure (like a school or a textbook). And where education spending is concerned, higher education and elite universities are the clear favorites.

Investment in infrastructure is only the most visible form of state support for private companies. All five countries also undertake serious efforts toward technology transfer. Precise arrangements differ but they share a relatively uniform pattern that combines funding government institutions, offering transnational enterprises attractive cooperation agreements, and sponsoring national champions. These national champions supply local marketing opportunities to their international partners and are therefore attractive to transnational companies in search of access to new markets. Transnational companies benefit from locally trained, yet still cheap labor in exchange for their knowledge of global business practice. National champions build on this knowledge, customizing it to local conditions so that subsequent local innovation can take off.

PROMOTING LEARNING

For national champions and other local firms, cooperation with transnational companies is essential. Even when there are no explicit knowledge-transfer provisions, transnational companies are forced to transfer at least some knowledge so that their local partners can execute orders. Much of this learning may even be informal, gained simply through exposure to transnational business practice. The same principle of knowledge transfer applies to global value chains consisting of purchaser-supplier relationships rather than joint venture partnerships. Value chains may have a very exploitative character in the distribution of the incomes that are generated by the chain, but local suppliers cannot be exploited by the dominant company which manages the chain without at the same time learning from their (often exploitative) transnational purchasers. Thus important knowledge is transferred down the chain even to erstwhile exploited participants in the value chain.

Learning in value chains can be supported by governments via direct subsidies (as has been done in the development of China's domestic auto industry) or indirectly by promoting research capacities in academic institutions connected to innovations (as is common in Brazil). The larger the stock of local knowledge, the easier it is to unpack imported technology. Even when local companies do not gain direct knowledge of how to solve industrial problems, indirect knowledge about solutions found elsewhere can increase their capacity to find different solutions that are not protected by intellectual property rights. The development of technical knowledge also facilitates "reverse engineering" as a major source for the development of local technology. Thus participation in global value chains is crucial as a form of learning-by-doing.

The general technical knowledge of local companies is improved by operating on the world market, and the greater their knowledge, the more flexible companies become in their own research and development. In particular they learn how to adjust imitated or purchased foreign technologies to local conditions. When dealing with the foreign economic policies of the BRICSs, we will show that they all engage in close relations with foreign transnational companies in order to increase knowledge transfers, despite the fact that these companies impose conditions for this cooperation. The BRICS countries also use the purchase of brownfield sites and loss-making foreign firms, especially those in advanced countries, to increase their knowledge and therefore their capacity for development.

The strategy of intensifying technology transfer appears in complete opposition to the previous development strategies that were pursued during the quest for a New International Economic Order in the 1970s. Then, transnational enterprises were expected merely to transfer technologies whole cloth, with technology considered a common heritage of humanity. The new strategy of the

BRICS countries in the 2000s consists in allowing transnational companies high short-term profits in exchange for long-term prospects for technology upgrading. Host countries cannot be certain of ultimately garnering the benefits of upgrading but can provide complementary political environments that improve their chances of benefiting from their deals with transnational companies.

Access to technology is facilitated by the size of the local market, which is where the BRICSs have a particular advantage over other developing countries. Foreign companies look to the BRICSs for economies of scale that can reduce their costs for products sold on the world market and increase their sales in the local markets they partner with. The larger the local market, the higher the negotiating power of the local government.

All five BRICS countries have deliberate policies of creating national innovation systems out of networks of universities, local administrations, and local private or state-owned companies. These institutions have developed in path-dependent ways that have been highly influenced by previous institutional arrangements particular to each country. The ultimate goal of these efforts, however, is always to build the capability of local firms to compete globally themselves. China, Brazil, and India have been so successful in this endeavor that some of their companies have been able to penetrate foreign markets, even developed country markets, often with explicit government financial support.

USING COMPARATIVE ADVANTAGE FOR UPGRADING

The electronics industry has played a major role. This is a technology family which has emerged recently where the newly industrializing countries (NIC), to which the BRICSs belong, started not far behind the old industrialized countries. As the technology in electronics is relatively recent, there are fewer differences in learning-by-doing between old industrialized countries and newcomers. Both new and old industrialized countries have been active in electronics production for a relatively short time. In some older technologies, productivity backwardness runs much deeper. Differences in experience from leaning-by-doing are high because of a complete absence of production in the NICs of such industries. The strong presence of NICs in high-tech industries contrasts with their simultaneous dependency on technology imports for the high-technology branches, especially in the case of China. There, high-technology exports constitute an important share of value creation despite low local shares of just 25 percent of value added.

The strong presence of China and India (and to a lesser extent Brazil) in high-technology industries is remarkable. Some of these are visible on consumer markets, such as (generic) medical products for mass consumption, consumer electronics including laptops and personal computers, and software development. Other industries that are more removed from household consumption, like nuclear and space technology, are also well developed, with China and India now following Russia and Brazil. In the cases of China, India, and Brazil this high-technology performance is not linked to a previous period of state-dominated superpower industrialization as it is in Russia.

This relatively higher competitiveness in new industries contradicts popular theories of the product cycle and polarization in technical competence. The BRICSs tend to stay away from old industries and specialize in the most modern branches. The traditional theory of international specialization in the context of product cycle models is not exactly wrong: some growth processes do confirm a pattern in which newcomers specialize in old industries, for instance the entry into old industries via labor-intensive products like textiles, shoes, and toys. But these product cycle approaches to development seem increasingly anachronistic in the twenty-first century.

The BRICSs have benefited from product cycle specialization, but not in the direct sense implied by product cycle theories. In the BRICSs, employment creation by older technology branches through low-skilled labor-intensive procedures created an environment where at least in some isolated sites the absorptive capacity for most modern technology improved. Such increases resulted simultaneously in the host countries becoming more attractive for expanding production and in the reduction of costs for transnational enterprises. This new attractiveness brought with it an initially low, but rapidly increasing capacity for reverse engineering.

The problem with the product cycle approach to development is that success in the acquisition of simple technologies does not automatically lead to the spread of technological innovation throughout the whole production system. India and China have reached excellence in many technologies, but centers of innovation are highly regionally concentrated. The most modern sectors grow alongside much larger sectors of the economy that retain very low-level technologies operated by low-skilled labor.

DEVELOPING NEW INDUSTRIES

The challenge for state power in using rents to promote development is that development itself puts barriers in the way of the continued state utilization of rents. Developing with state support on the basis of profitability through the market tends to reinforce the political weight of the managerial class, that is owners or managers of private market-oriented companies. Managers of private market-oriented companies rarely have a view of the overall macroeconomic relations. They see costs—including especially the cost of labor in the wake of wage increases—primarily through the lens of their own profitability. To them, costs are nothing more than a drag on their profits and hence an obstacle to growth, whereas in reality the higher consumption that is made possible by higher wages is strongly beneficial for capitalist growth.

Giving political responsibility for the overall health of the economy to enterprise managers reinforces the self-centered positions

of companies and tends to lead inevitably toward austerity policies. But the factors that make a business successful are not the
same as those that make an economy successful. Thus business
managers should not have economic decision-making power in a
capitalist economy. The health of a capitalist economy as a whole
basically depends on the balance between a cost-reducing capitalist class and a consumption-increasing working class, and politi-
cians must represent that larger working class in order for the
whole system to prosper.

Unfortunately, in developing transition societies the currently
dominant austerity theories of development tend to go unchal-
lenged. This is partly due to an underdeveloped civil society (especially in the case of communist and postcommunist countries like
China and Russia) but also due to the absence of strong shop-
floor and street-side opposition from labor. Theoretical debates
in all of the BRICS countries (except perhaps South Africa) show
an absence of explanations based on a mixed economy and real
economy-oriented Keynesian principles. Instead they stretch only
as far as an interest in monetary policy and monetary Keynesian-
ism. Export dependence makes an exclusive focus on investment
appear practicable, at least as long as external markets are absorptive. China's transition to increased internal development in the
last decade shows the contradictions of such an approach.

When the focus is on the primacy of investment, the social
developments that result from successful industrialization constitute a further obstacle to the all-important shift to more egalitarian development. This is because success in development liberates
the asset-owning classes from the limits to growth imposed by
underdevelopment. Brazil's shift to the primacy of industrial sectors oriented primarily to care for mass needs under the workers'
party was only made possible by divisions within the asset-owning
class and the emergence of a new stratum of entrepreneurs influenced by the social doctrines of the Catholic Church. Today, after
much successes in development, this alliance between the workers'

party and the more progressive tendencies among the business class appears to have broken down.

The frailty of alliances which promote a shift from the supply-side start of accumulation to a complementary expansion of internal mass demand is more problematic given that rents increase (and by dint of that the incentive for rent hoarding among owners) in the wake of the initial successes of such efforts. So in Brazil the much-hailed expansion of mass consumption (and concomitant reduction in poverty) produced greater opportunities for rent extraction by Brazilian companies, opportunities they now seek to lock in through austerity policies that will limit future development. The same pressure is being felt in China under the rubric of accepting the "new normal" of lower taxes and slower growth.

Historically, rents were available in the BRICSs because of the precapitalist power structures that allowed surplus to be appropriated by political means without any consideration for economic competitiveness. The splendid courts of the older empires in Asia, pre-Columbian America, and to some extent in sub-Saharan Africa provide testimony of the availability of rents. These less developed countries were and still are characterized by differences in lags in productivity in relation to the industrial center. They are not uniformly behind, so their backwardness in productivity does vary according to production lines: high backwardness in manufacturing but low backwardness, if any, in raw material production, where sometimes, due to depletion of rich raw material deposits in the industrialized world, underdeveloped economies are even more productive in absolute terms.

Today, becoming competitive in new manufacturing production lines requires overcoming low levels of experience in production and low economies of scale resulting from initially low production runs. Increasing production and benefiting from learning-by-doing can be expected to reduce average and marginal costs of production in backward countries much more than in developed countries. Developing countries may want to increase their exports by lowering their prices, and they may use government resources for that purpose. But at some level their exports will no longer increase much even if prices continue to fall. For example, South Korea quickly became so competitive in textile production that it was supplying large parts of the world market; it experienced declining price elasticity of demand when prices fell more rapidly than quantities were increasing.

The newly industrializing countries and the BRICSs are often specialized in products with low price elasticity of demand, at least in the case of a massive increase of export quantities as markets become saturated. Their earnings often will not increase in line with increasing exports because of unfavorable price effects. Reducing quantities exported may make sense if prices increase more rapidly than quantities have to fall. These countries will cream off rents from the branches where the products are already competitive on the world market at relatively high prices. This money can then be used for diversification of production into new production lines which are not yet competitive. The strategy can seem counterintuitive for any one firm, but it often makes sense for industries taken as a whole.

For example, finding its textile exports limited by a saturated market, South Korea blocked the import of textile machinery and launched initially high-cost local textile machinery production. This production became the basis of a diversified machine tool industry. Similar instruments to upgrade production include local content rules, export taxes, and obligations for training workers. They all apply the same type of mechanism: "artificially" (i.e., state-imposed) increased costs in branches of industry that can bear such costs in order to appropriate rents in the form of taxes for subsidizing diversification to other industries. This imposes added expenses on highly price-competitive industries in order to promote other industries and achieve industrial diversification.

For countries that pursue this kind of rent-driven strategy, the rents generated by the economy will increase over the long term.

Rents will not be eliminated until high levels of employment in the modernizing sector of the economy are achieved to such an extent that labor scarcity manifests itself even in the less dynamic sectors of the economy, like traditional agriculture and traditional services. South Korean economists categorized those pressures as the turning point of export-oriented industrialization as a means of overcoming underdevelopment. There may be real wage increases even before full employment among the labor force trained for the highly productive, mostly export-oriented branches of production, but when wage increases become generalized and independent from the specific level of productivity of the different sectors of the economy (e.g., when even the wages of hairdressers and agricultural laborers catch up), the turning point has been reached.

As long as labor is not scarce, there will be little spillover of wage increases from the highly competitive branches of the economy to the rest of the economy. In capitalism, wage increases follow average productivity, not branch-specific productivity, because workers are mobile across sectors. The coevolution of wage increases in branches with low productivity increases and branches with high productivity increases is the political-economic basis of the formation of a working class. As capitalism depends for its good operation on the countervailing power of labor against business, there is no automatic establishment of capitalism until structural unemployment is absorbed. Supply-side growth on the basis of accumulation from rents and the construction of new enterprises does not invariably lead to the formation of capitalist social and economic structures. During the process, blockages may occur if the supply-side element of the process, though successfully realized, is not complemented by the socioeconomic empowerment of labor.

The availability of foreign technology intensifies this contradiction because it allows rapid increases of productivity in some sectors without other sectors necessarily following. Additionally, the availability of imported technology does not necessarily create jobs or increases in investment in local goods production: the increasing scope for economies of scale that comes in the wake of more productive technology might not be sufficiently exploited under an absence of additional demand, even from the higher-skilled labor in the more advanced sectors of the economy. Economies of scale require mass consumption, which requires high incomes, which requires full employment throughout the economy, not just in the most advanced sectors.

The increasing negotiating power of the large developing countries (such as the BRICSs) that host transnational enterprises under a guarantee of short-term profits for the locally operating transnationals implies that host countries tend to follow "reasonable" macroeconomic policies, namely "healthy" fiscal policies with respect to debt and the exchange rate. This increases the host country's leverage in its dealings with the transnationals on the conditions of acquiring technology. Host countries which tolerate labor agitation, budget deficits for employment creation, or the threat of devaluation decrease this leverage.

This does not imply that transnationals oppose social reform, but social reform imposed by popular protest is another dimension. Keeping social reform under control by limited political participation works better than open class struggles for gaining transnational companies' trust. But the dominant ideology of the priority of investment and denying the relevance of mass consumption does not supply strong arguments for such preemptive social reform. Ironically, what business needs most is what businesses universally resist: government intervention to improve workers' conditions and, crucially, pay.

STATE INTERVENTION AND THE INTERNATIONAL DIMENSION

The state is quite capable of managing rent in supply-side-oriented processes of growth. This capacity of the state appears as the result of the accumulation of surplus. The efficiency of capitalism, and hence the capitalistically managed modern sector of the economy, is due to the fact that capitalist entrepreneurs have to use capital parsimoniously. Even high rates of accumulation and high shares of investment spending in gross national product do not contribute enough to ensure the rapid absorption of structural unemployment.

Access to the international market is therefore essential, and trade surpluses are a major instrument for increasing employment without parallel increases in rent collection by the privileged strata. Nonetheless, in such a transitional process the world market is not large enough to absorb enough exports from all of the still-underdeveloped world to create enough jobs that will bring all of the world's poor into prosperous full employment. This limits the impact of exports in socially transforming the hitherto underdeveloped world. Solely mobilizing labor for exports is worthwhile but not enough. The more the respective countries succeed in supply-side growth, the more problems this creates for the absorptive capacity on the outside world.

Exacerbating this problematic, in processes of supply-side-oriented growth the forces that oppose redistribution are strengthened, whereas the forces which try to organize to impose redistribution remain weak. Catch-up industrialization does not automatically trigger the kinds of demand-side policies that are necessary to make this type of industrialization sustainable. In only two of the five BRICS countries, Brazil and South Africa, has labor been able to constitute itself as an independent political force that is able to maintain an active political dialog with the state. In Brazil, the weakness of labor has been demonstrated by the recent crisis; in South Africa, an originally highly revolutionary labor organization which was the backbone of the national liberation struggle has been co-opted by a rent-collecting state class.

None of the five BRICS countries has undergone the process of mobilizing labor independently of skills in mass collective unions of the kind that once flourished in today's developed countries, a process that was essential for the emergence of modern capitalism toward the end of the nineteenth century. Where labor mobilization has occurred in the developing countries of today, the emerging organizations have often focused more on controlling labor (and labor unrest) than on enabling labor's resistance to exploitation and unfair practices. In China this process is so far advanced that the unions themselves (such as they are) are parts of the state administration.

Therefore the role of the state in a catching-up process is important, and contradictory. It is very positive with respect to the capacity of mobilizing resources and engaging in supply-side strategies when it limits itself to mobilizing otherwise unemployed resources. If the capitalist growth mechanism is absent or blocked, a market-oriented competitive capitalist sector cannot absorb all potentially available surplus: the alternative is not between market or state, but between a market complemented by state mobilization of surplus in the form of rent accruing to a more or less centralized agent (i.e., the state or agencies of the state), or a market characterized by underemployment with rents accruing to private interests who have every incentive to transfer their capital abroad (i.e., out of reach of the state).

Developing profit by extending mass demand and creating a local investment goods industry is difficult because it implies relatively far-reaching social change. Improving conditions of production by state investment, even if as rents, is less efficient than increasing production through private investment. Private investment, if profitable (which requires sufficient demand), is easier to implement and can be hoped to ultimately produce higher levels of employment and, through this, greater empowerment of labor as well. These pressures tend to push governments to use rents for the protection of existing industries instead of for the support of innovation. Still, in the absence of increasing mass demand, direct state investment in the economy is superior to letting private firms limit investment to those activities that are already profitable.

The effective direction of state investment depends on the efficiency and the dedication of nonmarket-controlled "elites" and appropriate arrangements for combining market with nonmarket forms of managing surplus. These are various forms of control for keeping the self-privileging of such elites within bounds. Singapore is perhaps the country that has been most successful at achieving such a balance. Its strategy has been to invest in multiple state-owned or state-directed companies that compete against each other. While it may seem technically inefficient for the state to compete against itself, this strategy generates the major positive externality whereby the managers of state-owned enterprises in Singapore mimic the behavior of privately owned companies.

Simultaneous steering by markets and the state, based on profit complemented by rent, requires an alliance between market and rent-oriented agents, an alliance under the permanent danger of market-oriented agents protecting themselves by means of political negotiation from the discipline imposed by the market. There must be a permanent struggle at a higher level against this tendency, for example through standing anticorruption campaigns and public review board oversight. The ultimate success of the imposition of market discipline depends on strengthening the one element that is absent in as-yet noncapitalist structures: that is, the empowerment of labor.

The issue for the role of the state is how to transform the available surplus from rents into profits by mobilizing this surplus in the form of rent by state power and allocating it to investment which promotes market structures and strengthens market-oriented elements, without totally submitting to the habitual primacy of the market. For such a process, there is no self-reinforcing mechanism beyond the possible (but not guaranteed) strength of supply-side-triggered accumulation leading to very high levels of employment, where labor feels itself so scarce that it becomes capable of transforming mere sporadic resistance into true nationwide organizations. In achieving such levels of organization, labor can negotiate the conditions of its exploitation in a way that marries its own increasing consumption with the stabilization of capitalism and the limitation of the privileges and prerogatives of business.

Even without the positive role of the state, and even without the empowerment of labor, we can imagine the very success of economic growth leading to situations where economic and social systems become extremely stable with rent shared in the form of limited concessions to labor, where waste emerging from luxury consumption patterns is at least somewhat limited, and where the society is organized harmoniously following the precapitalist principle of "to each his due." Such a structure can be further stabilized also by means of nationalism. This scenario perfectly describes contemporary China, which after four decades of rapid growth seems to be stabilizing in a new social compact that subsidizes the profitability of inefficient state-owned enterprises while guaranteeing minimum wages and basic services to most workers. However, economic growth has stalled.

The credibility and the social impact of nationalist ideologies might increase by the tendencies of multilateral power competitions internationally, which the rise of the BRICSs will trigger. The rise of the BRICSs is embedded in an international polity where previous major powers feel threatened and where rising new major powers (the BRICSs) have to carve out their place in the international decision-making bodies. Four of the five BRICSs are pervaded with nationalist ideologies of some hue or another: in China, they have a secular tinge; in India, they are shared between secular nationalists and cultural nationalists; in Russia, nationalism has become a major instrument for stabilizing "guided democracy"; in South Africa, nationalism allows the African National Congress to maintain its power despite relatively meager results in economic and social transformation. Only in Brazil is nationalism seemingly receding, where the decline of the alliance between enlightened business and labor is piloted by the resurgence of an openly reactionary cosmopolitan elite.

The contradictions inherent in the role of the state for catching up imply that the winning policy of redistributing income in the process of economic growth is rarely chosen, and that when it is chosen (as it has been until recently in Brazil) it is politically unstable. Policies that promote the downward redistribution of income could be made easier to implement if it could be demonstrated that such policies foster growth. By creating internal markets constituted by larger mass incomes, states can increase investment opportunities, profits can grow, and local technological development can be promoted. But this leap of faith, which is necessary to escape the middle-income trap, has rarely been made intentionally by a government in the self-conscious pursuit of economic growth.

3 MASS DEMAND AS THE BASIS OF GROWTH

Technical progress, the ultimate basis of economic growth, consists in reducing the effort required to make existing products and in the discovery of new products. Both processes are facilitated by rising mass incomes and increasing costs for unskilled and semi-skilled labor. If there is technical progress in a certain activity, costs of production are likely to go down and enterprises will try to expand their markets by reducing prices. If they succeed, production and employment in this activity increase. In cases of high overall levels of employment, wages may also increase in activities where no technical progress has occurred. Suppose that there is an increase of demand for labor in an innovative activity. Noninnovative activities will lose labor. They can only be maintained if wages increase there as well, and this may become possible because total output in the noninnovative activities will decrease so that prices per unit produced can increase as some demand is not satisfied. Increases in labor costs in noninnovative branches may just be the result of technical progress elsewhere in the economy that pushes up the general wage level of the country as a whole.

The increasing expense for low or average skilled labor justifies the search for new technical solutions, solutions that often demand the employment of higher-skilled labor. As average skilled labor or labor with obsolete skills becomes more expensive, it becomes worthwhile to expand the use of the kinds of high-performing skilled labor associated with costly technical solutions that would have been prohibitive when unskilled labor was still cheap.

The ubiquity of technical progress in capitalist economies is ultimately the result of scarce labor and wages that rise due to the empowerment of labor. High mass incomes and high economies of scale resulting from large and relatively homogeneous markets make it possible for companies to search for solutions by reducing costs through mass production. They also promote the search to control increasing labor costs that have risen due to productivity increases in other sectors or labor-costs rises in branches where technical progress was initially sluggish. Finding solutions to particular problems leads to a widespread capacity to apply new technology in the most varied parts of the economy. This is greatly promoted by high costs of labor and the concomitant high demand for average-quality products for average consumers. Catching-up economies therefore have to create mechanisms that keep income distribution relatively egalitarian while still creating incentives for innovation and entrepreneurship. The empowerment of labor on the labor market is an effective way to ensure its participation in the fruits of technical progress.

Rising prices for products where little technical progress has occurred, and declining prices for innovative products with dynamically expanding markets, will lead to relatively similar levels of productivity and wages across the economy and, ultimately, to high flexibility as innovative activities with expanding demand attract labor from less innovative ones. Increases in productivity in innovative activities tend to be lower in monetary terms than in physical terms because enterprises that are involved in innovative activities are thus able to use part of the increase in physical productivity to reduce prices in order to attract new consumers.

Wage rates and profit rates thus tend to converge between new and old branches. There is an important implication of this: under conditions of full employment, working conditions and the remuneration of labor do not vary much for very long between different activities. The relatively homogeneous conditions for labor allow its transformation into a politically active working class with similar and economically focused demands (good wages, moderate hours of work, job security, etc.). This allows local labor combativeness to coexist with the large-scale, ideally nationwide, organization of labor as a counterpart of capital. The convergence of labor incomes across an entire economy facilitates the emergence of relatively high income shares for labor (generating mass demand), large markets for identical products, and economies of scale. Under these conditions, mass production techniques are a major source of productivity growth. And productivity growth reduces costs.

The key here is full employment. Without government policies that promote full employment, the game is lost. When government-sponsored programs for technical improvement are not complemented by the effects of increasing homogeneous mass demand, the cost-reducing effect of economies of scale only operates in export-oriented branches. Technical progress can take place in highly inegalitarian societies, but due to the absence of mass demand, progress focuses on the excellence of the single product without spillover to the rest of the economy. This has occurred since ancient times, when highly unequal ancient empires achieved impressive technical and artistic excellence in specific fields without experiencing generalized economic development. The same was true in the noncapitalist economies of the twentieth century, for example when both Nazi Germany and the Soviet Union excelled in particular technologies without being able to provide prosperity for the whole of their societies. And this process is occurring in the BRICSs today, which host many leading export industries (civilian aircraft in Brazil, military aircraft in Russia, business process outsourcing in India, infrastructure in China, mining in South Africa) but have not generalized technical progress throughout their economies.

Economies with high levels of employment and rising mass demand are characterized by high levels of investment spending because companies in all branches of production are incentivized to invest to improve productivity. The link between rising mass incomes, relatively homogeneous mass demand, and high levels of investment is at the heart of our argument that profitability of the system as a whole is linked to mass demand and the capitalist system itself is grounded in the empowerment of labor. It is exactly this link which the BRICSs have had trouble exploiting.

The three BRICS countries with relatively better economic performance—China, India, and Brazil—have to some extent tried to maintain profitability through mass demand by implementing policies that at least partially favor the poor, but all three have stopped well short of the full empowerment of labor and all three still have extraordinarily unequal distributions of income. By contrast, the developing countries that succeeded in breaking through the middle-income trap (Japan, South Korea, and Taiwan) all pursued radical agrarian reforms at the beginning of their export drives and all have very strong national labor movements. Export orientation is a good first step for economic development, but without the empowerment of labor the success of export industries does not spill over into the economy at large.

INCREASING MASS INCOMES BY MOBILIZING RENTS

The BRICSs share with other underdeveloped economies characteristics that block high levels of employment. Development scholars have historically called this the problem of surplus labor in underdeveloped economies. The basic outline of the theory of surplus labor in underdeveloped economies can be summarized as the existence of marginality: labor that produces less than it needs to consume. Such low-productivity labor is essentially unemployable.

This theory goes back to the midtwentieth-century economist Nicholas Georgescu-Roegen and was applied in Indian debates on the link between the small size and high yields of peasant farms. Due to demographic growth, more and more labor was applied to a limited amount of arable land; the increasingly unfavorable combination between labor and land leads to diminishing returns. Demographic growth continued as long as the redistributive mechanisms of precapitalist societies were still functioning within the village communities and the extended families. At some point the additional product of additional workers is lower than the additional resources needed to support those workers, but as long as traditional, precapitalist mechanisms of surplus distribution are in place the workers continue to get fed. But when capitalist labor relations are introduced, marginal workers are shed (marginalized) and they have to search for other work on the labor market.

In such conditions, structural unemployment emerges. Structural unemployment does not allow any negotiating power for workers, even of workers with average skills who in principle produce more than they consume, because there is always a surplus of other desperate workers willing to displace them. The mechanism through which the scarcity of labor empowers workers, so essential for the transition to capitalism in the eighteenth and nineteenth centuries, is absent. Just as state-led, import-substituting industrialization did not create conditions for the empowerment of labor in the underdeveloped world in the twentieth century, the shift to more market-oriented strategies today still has to deal with the problem of the underemployment of labor. It does not generate sufficient employment growth for the mass of labor to enable it to negotiate over the distribution of the fruits of innovation and progress.

The BRICS countries have applied a variety of instruments for dealing with labor surpluses in ways that corresponded to their internal political power configurations. All such attempts ultimately depend on the mobilization of rents. Rural rents derived from agriculture are often the easiest to mobilize, but today's underdeveloped countries often have other rents they can use as well. For example, raw material endowments (e.g., Russia and South Africa), strategic locations (e.g., Egypt and Panama), and even labor-intensive manufactured exports (e.g., Singapore and Korea in their periods of rapid development) can all generate rents that can then be used to absorb surplus labor.

In the twentieth century most countries of the South and all of the BRICs followed some form of state-led import-substitution industrialization, and all failed to develop due to their failure to shift their industries to serve local and international mass markets. The small number of local high-income consumers in the BRICS countries led to an orientation of production toward low batch (and therefore high-cost) production with low spillovers into local technology production. This was most extreme in the case of China, where giant auto factories employing tens of thousands of workers turned out just a few hundred cars a year, all bound for use by party cadres. Similar (though less extreme) outcomes prevailed in the other BRICS countries as well.

In the twenty-first century the BRICS countries shifted to various degrees of export orientation combined with efforts to increase the incomes of the rural poor. Agrarian reform gave the peasantry access to the market in China; in India, limited agrarian reform in favor of middle peasants with redistributional systems in favor of the very poor (including labor procurement programs managed by nongovernmental organizations) were implemented; in Brazil, conditional income redistribution was made famous by the Bolsa Familia; and in post-apartheid South Africa, cash payments in favor of the "deserving" poor (while withholding resources from the unemployed able-bodied poor) were implemented. Even in Russia the traditional Soviet welfare state continued to some extent (though with large gaps), especially with respect to rural pensioners.

Though most international and scholarly attention has focused on the export-openness side of the equation, most of the (limited) success of the BRICS economies would not have been possible without their policies to raise the incomes of the rural poor. The

admiration of the BRICS economies is largely linked to the aston-
ishing performance of China and to a lesser extent of India, both
having grown out of dire poverty less than five decades ago. Given
their population, economic growth in these two countries has
added more to world income in the last five decades than did the
industrialization of the West between 1820 and 1950. But the two
cases of China and India do not conform to the mainstream inter-
pretation of development and transition to capitalism that suggests developing countries must maximize the available surplus for
investment by reducing consumption as much as possible. Both
countries have undertaken, with admittedly different success, substantial redistributive measures in order to strengthen popular
consumption and well-being.

In China, food self-sufficiency during the reform period was
essential for shifting to export-led industrialization based on the
devaluation of the Yuan. The low Yuan in effect cheapened the
international price of Chinese labor by means of an exchange rate
below purchasing power parity with other currencies. At an
exchange rate below purchasing parity, export earnings are lower
than the equivalent world market price of the products that are still
being consumed locally for the reproduction of labor. With a high
share of food in the total consumption of poor households, success
in domestic agricultural production is a precondition for successful
export-oriented manufacturing whenever large-area countries are
involved. Chinese export industries still depend to a very large
extent on foreign technology, especially in the technically more
demanding lines of production, but the reliance on imported components (like touch screens and semiconductors) is sustainable
because the real, international prices of products imported from
abroad do not change when a country devalues its currency.

The political economy of egalitarian land reform can be summarized as integrating marginal labor into production despite its
relatively low productivity. In the case of rural producers having
approximately the same endowment in productive land, all house-

holds will have some highly productive work time but also additional working hours which do not add as much to overall production. They will achieve relatively high yields in the first hours of their workday, but as long as they have no better ways to increase their earnings, they will continue to work on their farms even as their productivity falls. As a result, labor productivity decreases but yields per hectare increase, and so total production increases (the essential target to meet in a poor society).

Without any further intervention such a relatively egalitarian agricultural system supplies additional labor to industry when nonagricultural activities start to pay higher wages than the decreasing marginal product in agriculture. This is the economic foundation for the expansion of rural by-employment in industry, as evidenced in 1980s China in female employment in small- and medium-scale industries and in the rise of township and village enterprises (TVEs). Migrant workers, particularly women, moved from low-productivity agriculture to more rapidly growing branches in the 1980s, not because they were destitute but because they were searching for higher incomes. Their continuing property rights in land would allow them to return to the countryside if incomes in the city fell. The higher incomes of permanent city dwellers do not block this mechanism of increasing mass incomes through migration. Overcoming economic marginality does not necessarily imply the achievement of full equality.

India was not able to enact such far-reaching redistribution of land as China did under communism, and thus India's postliberalization reforms have been more limited than China's. In India the richer strata of the peasantry are an important part of the interclass coalition on which the Congress Party as a national liberation movement was based. Agrarian reform was therefore limited. Rich landlords, the so-called Zamindari, who originated as the tax collectors of the Mughal period and were transformed into estate owners by the colonial state, were to some extent expropriated and could keep only part of their land with ceilings fixed at relatively high levels. Further land redistribution was thwarted, as landlords distributed land within their large families to members without much land or to their own children. As a result, in major parts of India middle peasants became dominant and opposed any further changes in power and property structures in favor of the poor.

Nevertheless, in some areas land distribution became more egalitarian than in others. There were historical factors: the occupation of India by colonial powers proceeded in steps, starting mostly from the eastern side of the peninsula (because of the importance of Bengal for the early colonial state). With increasing administrative penetration, the British colonial administration of India shifted its method of guaranteeing political stability from an alliance with the former tax collectors of the Mughal state (who had been transformed by the so-called permanent settlement of 1793 into estate owners) to direct administrative tax collection from individual nuclear-family peasant households, the ryots. In the newly occupied regions of the west of India, like the Punjab, Indian agriculture was transformed into owner-operated smallholder agriculture.

Because of the limits to the redistribution of land, independent India reinvigorated a very old Indian tradition of voluntary social work organizations in the form of modern NGOs that extensively complement the public sector. There are many Indian NGOs, but data on their performance are limited and contradictory. Two domains of NGO activity are central for poverty reduction: the public distribution system (PDS) and rural employment programs.

The PDS distributes essential commodities (especially rice and wheat but in some places also edible oils and basic vegetables) to households below and slightly above the poverty line via so-called fair price shops. Needy households receive a ration card, which plays the role of a national identity card for the poor. Amounts distributed are scheduled to cover the basic needs of poor households, but real deliveries are much too small. As a result the reduction in food prices relative to the free market does not sensibly improve the income situation of the poor in the large majority of the districts of India. A lack of central government funding made state governments cut back these programs to levels where households can buy only a minor proportion of their necessities at the reduced rates offered in fair price shops, about 3 percent in all.

The unemployed poor, especially in the countryside, also benefit by working in government-sponsored employment programs. The Mahatma Gandhi National Rural Employment Guarantee Act centralized a previously dispersed system of food-for-work programs. This law guarantees one hundred workdays per year to one member of each nuclear family. Anyone who is not offered a job is entitled after fifteen days to unemployment benefits. Between forty-five and fifty-five million families have benefited from this program in recent years. The poorest groups in India, the so-called scheduled tribes and scheduled castes, benefit disproportionately, as do poor women. Employment programs have a long tradition in independent India as a form of mobilizing underemployed labor. They address the root cause of underdevelopment: marginality and the lack of negotiating power among unskilled labor.

Although the Indian employment programs have contributed to the improvement of infrastructures in the countryside (schools, roads, wells, etc.), their contribution on the supply side of economic development is far less important than equivalent policies that could create demand for labor by rendering labor competitive in dynamic markets. The result would be creating household purchasing power at the lower levels of income capable of significant material improvement. The share of rural people living in modern houses is more than twice as high in China as in India, where even poor city dwellers often live in shacks in shantytowns. Because India has failed relative to China in the redistribution of rural assets (land), the much weaker dynamics of growth in export manufacturing in India are not soaking up India's excess rural labor supply. The link between export growth and internal market development is thus much more tenuous in India than in China.

Brazil is the only one among the BRICS countries where no revolutionary change has impacted the extremely unequal precapitalist distribution of land. Brazilian landlordism and the oligarchical structures built upon it—even in the urban world—were not broken up when capitalist relations of production began to penetrate the country in the first part of the twentieth century. Due to the sheer size of Brazil's internal market, a highly elite-oriented import-substitution industrialization was relatively successful in job creation and led to the emergence of an urban working class in the 1940s. But without a dynamic internal mass market, and with increasing divergence between the interests of business and labor, the emerging organization of labor (ultimately coalescing in the Workers' Party) was for a long time unable to impose a center-left moderate government.

This configuration prevented the Workers' Party from engaging in a struggle for land redistribution, thereby alienating one of its original support groups, the highly visible landless workers' movement (the Movimento dos Trabalhadores Rurais Sem Terra, or MST). The MST was not served by the workers' movement, and the four million rural households the MST attempted to mobilize were left behind. When the Workers' Party was finally able to form a government in 2003, its social policies had as their centerpiece conditional cash payments in the form of the Bolsa Familia program. The Bolsa Familia is globally admired for moving forty-six million people out of extreme poverty and boosting immunization rates to 99 percent at a cost of less than half a percent of GDP. The Bolsa Familia is a direct cash transfer program, conditional on the recipient family's participation in prenatal care, immunization, and attendance at school. In the 2010s nearly a quarter of the population and essentially 100 percent of all households below the poverty line benefited from the Bolsa Familia. It is widely lauded as one of the great success stories of poverty reduction.

The impact of redistributive measures and the state-supported promotion of minimum living standards cost India and Brazil (and other leading countries of the Americas, like Mexico) between 0.5 and 1 percent of their gross domestic product. The fact that these transfers were so affordable implies, however, that their contribution to an expansion of the internal mass market was limited. They may have brought people out of poverty, but they have not served as the basis for launching local industries. In both Brazil and India, exports have been more important for raising ordinary people's purchasing power than has been the mobilization of mass incomes. Ironically, this has limited their prospects for development compared to China (an exporting powerhouse) because in Brazil and India export growth has not been accompanied by a commensurate expansion in domestic markets.

The two other BRICS countries, Russia and South Africa, may not have been among the top performers of the BRICSs but they have still done relatively well in boosting their export performance. This export performance has, however, remained limited because those countries allowed their successful natural resource exports to drive up the values of their currencies. This phenomenon is known as the "Dutch disease," a situation in which high earnings from raw material exports choke off success in other branches of manufacturing. Their export earnings kept the Russian and South African governments from suffering serious fiscal shortages and allowed them to use natural resource rents to pacify their populations. But both countries failed to use natural resource rents to generate mass domestic demand. Structural changes, especially agrarian reform or manufacturing export drives on the basis of low exchange rates, have not been attempted.

MIXING REDISTRIBUTION AND EXPORT-BASED GROWTH

Among the BRICSs only Brazil, India, and China represent cases that could, at least in part, guide the policies of other underdeveloped countries. Their main points of convergence are the mobilization of rent for employing otherwise marginal labor and the massive mobilization of rents in export-oriented industries through basically market-guided mechanisms. This keeps corruption in check in the state-dependent aspects of rent mobilization in export-oriented industries because they must innovate to keep up with competition on the world market.

Alongside agrarian reform and state-guided investment, export-oriented manufacturing (or, uniquely in India, services) is a key mechanism of rent mobilization in the BRICS economies. The basic mechanism consists in subsidizing labor, which given its low productivity does not produce a surplus beyond its bare costs of subsistence. All economies of the Global South that have been successful in raising productivity and employment through exports growth have kept their exchange rates below purchasing parity with major currencies. In the 1990s, a Beijing worker could buy four to nine times the amount of goods in China compared to the purchasing power of the same salary if it was converted into international currencies and used on international markets. Even today Chinese workers can still buy nearly twice as much on local markets as on international markets with the same income. In India the equivalent multiple is nearly three times.

At such an undervalued exchange rate the share of export earnings available for paying salaries to the workers is extremely limited, since a large part of the value of exported products consists of previously imported components. These components cannot easily be replaced by local products through devaluation. They are not locally produced, so access to cheaper labor is little help. These products do not become cheaper for the exporting economy through devaluation but have to be bought at their world market prices from the export proceeds of products, the export price of which had been reduced through devaluation. As a result, devaluation reduces the share of workers' remuneration in total export earnings. It is the workers' share of earnings that has to bear the bulk of the adjustment of export revenues.

Consequently, the bulk of the physical counterpart to workers' lost wages has to come from the local economy. These products, like food, textiles, household equipment, furniture, and basic "modern" products like refrigerators, television sets, stoves, and telephones, have to be purchased by the workers in the export sector. Most of these products are locally produced in the export-oriented BRICSs, so the expansion of the production of these items requires once more only an increase of the surplus to be drawn from local food production. It does not require large amounts of foreign currency.

Mobilizing rents for overcoming underdevelopment is not fundamentally different in strategies aimed at increasing exports versus strategies aimed at developing internal mass consumption. In both cases the increase of local food production is decisive. The three relatively successful BRICSs—China, India, and Brazil—succeeded in the green revolution and had become self-sufficient in food consumption long before any substantial increases in their real wages as a result of successful industrial development. Food came first and formed the basis for increasing the competitiveness of other industries, including higher technology.

The local surplus in food production was bought by the additional workers who came to be employed in the export manufacturing (or services) sectors, although their wages would not have been enough to buy the same foods on the world market. With export orientation, labor contributes in part to the maintenance of its wages, which also have to be complemented by the state for its survival. In the case of export orientation it is the blockage of local agriculture from the world market which keeps food prices low so that the export workers receive more food from their labor than their share in the income generated by the new exported products would provide them on the world market. The maintenance of workers capable of reacting to market demand channels this additional labor into occupations which ensure the highest possible level of social transformation through work in modern production lines. The big shift in moving from import substitution to export orientation is in the mechanism of monitoring and regulating this additional labor (the market rather than the state), not the origin of the resources they need to live (agricultural rents generated on the farm).

POSITIVE RESULTS IN STRENGTHENING CONSUMPTION BY THE POOR

The success of nonorthodox strategies for dealing with the challenge of underdevelopment is obviously apparent in the success of the BRICS countries (especially Brazil, India, and China) in improving their performance on the United Nations' Human Development Index (HDI). Between 1990 and 2014 the HDI improved spectacularly for China (1.58% per annum) and India (1.48% per annum), and a little less so for Brazil (0.91% per annum), whereas Russia and, even more, South Africa had poor performances despite initially high values. The improvement in HDI was most spectacular in China but was impressive in the three countries. By 2014 China had achieved 77 percent of the score of Norway (the top performer), Brazil 80 percent, and India 65 percent, all up substantially over the previous three decades.

This increase in material well-being in the best BRICS performers was reflected particularly in better nutrition: dietary energy supplies increased in China between 1992 and 2012 by 25 percent, in Brazil by 19 percent, and in India and South Africa by around 8 percent according to data from the United Nations Food and Agriculture Organization (FAO). Quality of food was improved as shown by a considerable increase of protein consumption, especially in China (from 65 to 89 grams per day), followed by Brazil (from 67 to 86 grams), South Africa (from 74 to 81 grams), and some way behind by India (from 55 to 58 grams). The share of cereals in people's diets declined massively, in China from 63 to 49 percent of total calories, and even in India from 64 to 58 percent.

Nevertheless, the basis of increased food intake was cereals, which may not be consumed directly but are instead fed to animals to produce higher-protein meats. Between 1961 and 2014 cereal production increased by factors of six in China, five in Brazil, and close to four in India. With the exception of Brazil (which has gone from being a grain importer to being a major agroindustrial exporter), annual per capita cereal production increased very slowly, in China from 371 to 399 kg in the thirty years from 1973 to 2013, and in India from 218 to 235 kg. Since the late 1990s, the rates of increase per capita production have declined and import requirements have tended to increase. China and India are actually involved in a race for agricultural land all over the world, especially in sub-Saharan Africa but also in Latin America.

On the basis of the improvement of the food situation for the mass of the population, poverty has declined. According to FAO data, the share of the poor in total population reached historically low levels, in Brazil 3.8 percent, in China 6.3 percent, in South Africa 9.4 percent, and in India 23.6 percent (judged in 2014 by the proportion of people living below the internationally accepted standard of $1.25 per day). This decline was particularly spectacular in China, where poverty has fallen by more than half, but Brazil has had similar success (reducing the share of the poor from 8.2% to 3.8%) and India has made substantial improvements (a reduction from 34.7% to 23.6%). These gains have come, however, without substantial reductions in income inequality across the economy as a whole. Wage inequality in particular remains extreme. In all BRICS countries except China, surpluses have been modestly mobilized to support policies that reduce poverty, but only in China have surpluses been aggressively mobilized to drive higher average wages.

Infrastructure has been greatly expanded, most dramatically in China. Good infrastructure can be even more important for the quality of life of the poor than of the rich, since the poor must rely on public services (e.g., grid electricity) while the rich can afford to provide for themselves (e.g., diesel generators). China has achieved the total electrification of the country and has realistic plans to connect every village in the country with paved roads by 2020. In Brazil near total electrification has been achieved, but there are still major pockets lacking infrastructure in both rural and urban areas, as there are in South Africa. Russia still relies on its overbuilt Soviet-era infrastructure but has put substantial resources into the construction of energy-related infrastructure. All of these are in marked contrast to India, where hundreds of millions of people are still at least partially excluded from modern power and transportation systems.

The evidence for human progress is contradictory beyond the fact that in Brazil, India, and China the supply of the basic necessities of life is ensured for the mass of the population by the government. This is especially true of food. To this extent the mix of different policies combining redistribution and employment growth has worked in all three cases of Brazil, India, and China. However, beyond such a minimum level of basic needs, the real integration of the mass of the population into production processes seems not to have succeeded in India and has succeeded only marginally in Brazil (considering its relatively higher initial level of development). In many segments of their economic and social structures there are massive pockets of poverty in India and Brazil, most visibly in their massive urban slums. South Africa and Russia have performed much less well at improving the lives of their poor, though of course South Africa started out with (and continues to have) much worse poverty than Russia.

The importance of increasing the incomes of the poor is much greater for today's catching-up economies than was historically the case of the Western industrialized countries: as productivity increases more rapidly in manufacturing than in other activities, latecomers have to apply the most modern technology very early in their development trajectories, and thus they produce more per capita in their manufacturing industries than early industrializers did. Today's late industrializers also have to contend with the fact that a more advanced outside world already exists and can be accessed by their own richest people. Since richer people have a higher tendency to consume imported manufactured products and a higher share of nonmanufactured products in their overall consumption, the already weaker impact of industrialization on the empowerment of labor will become weaker still if inequality increases.

THE CHINA DIFFERENCE

Obviously, the BRICS success is most pronounced in China. The question is less what mechanisms pushed the BRICSs to prominence than what mechanisms pushed China to prominence. One clear difference between China and the other BRICSs is the much greater export dynamism of China. It would, however, be wrong to deduce from this that internal structures are unimportant. Its superior export performance allowed China to dispense with costly administrative measures of surplus redistribution only because China had first implemented agrarian reform with land redistribution as a basic social security mechanism. In this, China was merely following the lead of Japan (under US administration), South Korea, and—ironically—Taiwan. In all of these Asian tigers, at the same time the export economy was growing and absorbing labor to produce additional exports, the more egalitarian internal structure provided workers with opportunities for negotiation in their favor.

Mass demand is central to the growth in the BRICSs, just as it was central to the growth of the Asian tigers before them. High shares of capital accumulation in national spending can be found elsewhere, such as in the oil-exporting countries. Investment alone is not enough to spark society-wide capitalist development. Among the newly industrializing export-oriented countries which do not belong to the BRICSs, exceptional growth rates were observed where the poor had better chances of their interests

being satisfied, as in South Korea and Taiwan; it is a process that
seems to be occurring now in Vietnam. Efforts for integrating
into the world market have been much less successful in countries
with less protection of the poor (like the Philippines). The economic empowerment of the poor is a key differentiating characteristic between the relatively successful and less successful
BRICSs just as it has been between the tiger economies and the
lagging economies of the Pacific Rim.

Rising mass income does not contradict the accumulation of
physical capital, because rising mass incomes can be paid for out
of unproductive rents, which are plentifully available in all underdeveloped countries. In well-functioning capitalist economies, rising mass incomes do not reduce profits, because any increase in
mass incomes on the basis of local production requires increasing
productive capacities, which are created by investment. Spending
more money on investment increases the rate of capital accumulation and hence also the rate of profit in any Keynesian modeliza-
tion of the economy, as demonstrated in the 1940s by Michal
Kalecki. Profit does not depend on the availability of financial
resources but on the use of available resources for spending on
investment. Empirical research has consistently shown that
increasing incomes drive private fixed-asset investment, not the
other way around.

The most successful economies of the Global South are those
that have been capable of channeling rents into support for
employment using market mechanisms instead of macroeconomic
state planning. It is, however, not market orientation per se which
produces rapid growth but the combination of a large variety of
measures for promoting employment of the mass of average
skilled labor. Old-fashioned state-promoted industrialization
requires high capacities for macroeconomic planning and is easily
vulnerable to implementation failures due to the opposition
between the interest of central planners in balanced development
and the interest of the executing agents (e.g., plant directors, local

administrators) in monopolizing resources under their own juris-
diction. And when people are judged on their success in meeting
arbitrary administrative targets, the prospect of widespread disin-
formation is always present.

Agrarian reform is politically difficult to implement because of
the defense of property rights by middle classes in the countryside, a policy equally supported by the middle classes in urban
areas. Similarly, currency devaluation is politically difficult because
it makes imported luxuries more expensive and it makes it more
difficult for the richer classes to travel (and spend) overseas.
Devaluation can also be resisted internationally as other countries
seek to protect their own markets from imports. The scarcity of
labor may have positive effects in strengthening the tendency
toward egalitarianism and the improvement of human capital, but
this can also be resisted by those who are currently at the top of
the national status hierarchy. And companies that are forced by
rising wages to improve their use of technology may be highly
resistant to being pushed to do so. All of these (counter-) forces
make it difficult for countries to pursue the policies outlined in
this chapter.

But in the long run (often after just a few years) even elites
benefit from the higher levels of economic development that can
be brought about through rapid demand-driven economic
growth. Rising mass incomes do not even require more equality in
the distribution of income if the economy is open to the world
market. Luxury imports for the rich can be paid for from the
exports of local industrial production and lead to high additional
employment despite inequality in the distribution of income. Just
look at China: the rich certainly have not suffered there.

The orientation of the local industrial sector to relatively simple
products, which even when more complex are regularly produced
in large quantities, allows the local production of both illegally
copied and legally imported goods. It also allows for improved
technology in local investment goods production. Rising mass

incomes can be achieved through a variety of measures, where exports of manufactured products, the protection of the poor through social programs, and state support for decisively important industries all play a role. That said, the reliance on mass consumption is the essential unifying element that drives capital accumulation, technical improvement, and the successful opening to the global market. You can't build a rich economy with only poor people. What most ideologically driven supply-side economists don't want to accept is that workers' compensation is not a passive factor in development. The empowerment of labor is what drives forward development within a well-institutionalized capitalist economy.

4 SELECTIVE LINKS TO

THE WORLD MARKET

The BRICs moniker may have been coined by an investment advisor, but the acronym gained such traction because the BRICS countries were emerging as new challengers in international relations and international politics. The never-ending obsession with the United States as the power at the apex of the world hierarchy aroused a macabre interest in its potential decline and decay due to the changing international division of labor. These new developments were seen as the result of the catching up in productivity of peripheries that were hitherto seen as backward and sometimes exotic. Economically, these developing peripheries were feared as challengers that threatened the competitiveness of American and European jobs. Politically, they constituted a danger to a world order which was imagined as just and natural by the reasonable citizens in the West.

The economic and political rise of the BRICSs—unforeseen by the mainstream liberal economists and Marxians alike—is just a manifestation of a well-functioning capitalist world economy. And in fact it is much less dramatic than it is usually portrayed (or feared) to be. The tendency of poorer countries to catch up with richer countries is much slower when it comes to technology than when looking just at overall levels of output. And the rise of global peripheries (including the BRICSs) does not constitute a danger for the Western style of life, even if labor in the Global South is very cheap. If anything, the rise of the rest helps subsidize Western ways of life. Even at the political level these countries do not threaten the security of the Western powers directly. They only challenge the pretentiousness of the West in claiming its right to impose its solutions wherever it desires in the rest of the world—and even then they often work in line with Western goals, not against them.

The new international division of labor is the fortunate result of capitalism, its tendency to allow all societies to take advantage of its decentralized nature and latecomers to develop on the basis not only of learning but also of overtaking established and heavily manageable societies. The process is not based on poverty and overexploitation of labor in the periphery or on preestablished hierarchical orders. Moreover, the process is not based on the illicit use of state power, although state power is used for accelerating it. If the process of catching up in industrial productivity and overall production is allowed to continue, it may under some circumstances even lead to a relatively harmonious development of countries in the direction of modern welfare states. The further development of capitalism in the BRICS countries does not have to lead to a beggar-thy-neighbor system of ever-lower labor standards, as critics suggest. In fact, labor standards have risen rapidly in Brazil and China over the last twenty years, and may be on the verge of improvement in South Africa.

International cooperation is an essential element for allowing underdeveloped countries to develop fully capitalist economies through the use of temporary export surpluses. This leads ultimately to more balanced relations in the international economy (and the wider interstate system) despite temporary imbalances created by government interventions in this process of the transition to capitalism. All of the BRICSs have used the world market as a tool for making their manufacturing more dynamic by accessing the larger pool of consumers that only the world market can provide, as the development economist A. P. Thirlwall has argued they should. Exports expanded at a breathtaking speed in the case of China (from 1995 to 2012 at 17% per annum) and are now growing even faster in India (19.3% per annum since 2005). These rates are considerably higher than the rate of increase for developing countries as a whole. The other three BRICSs have been less efficient. Their exports have grown at around the rate of developing countries as a whole, around 5 percent per year. As a result of these trends, the share of exports in national income has grown enormously in China and India. In China, exports went from next to nothing at the beginning of the reform era in 1978 to 35 percent in 2007 before cooling off after the global financial crisis. India's exports grew from around 5 percent of GDP in 1980 to a high of 25 percent in 2013. Since 2012, India's exports (as a percentage of GDP) have actually outstripped China's.

The BRICSs are not homogeneous with respect to their export success, but there are two giants: China and India. Russia's exports (as a percentage of GDP) are quantitatively in the same league but qualitatively very different, consisting almost entirely of oil, gas, and other mineral products. The same is true of South Africa, while Brazil—despite its recent soybean boom and bust—remains at levels last seen in China and India decades ago. China and India are still relatively poor (India being much poorer than China), whereas many other countries that have preceded them in export-oriented manufacturing have much higher average incomes and higher per capita exports, if slower growth. This suggests that there is still room even for China to continue to climb the export ladder. China's exports have been declining as a percentage of GDP since 2007 and in absolute terms since 2014, yet China is still nowhere near the income levels of East Asian export trailblazers like Japan, South Korea, and Taiwan. This suggests that it still has much room for export growth and that its 2015–16 strategy of currency appreciation is long premature.

The trajectories of China and India are linked to the growth of manufactured exports, though in India's case to services as well. Both have very high rates of growth of exports of all kinds of manufactured products, whereas the other three BRICSs have rates of only about two-thirds the average, albeit slightly increasing in the last decade. The share of the two Asian giants in total manufactured exports of the developing world increased from 15 percent in 1995 to 42 percent in 2012, though it must be said that the vast majority of this total came from China. India has begun to climb the same ladder as China, but it is on a much lower rung. In terms of economic structure, there is no such thing as a "BRICS economy." Instead there are China and India following the path first opened by the East Asian tiger economies, while the other three are stuck in relative economic stasis. Brazil, Russia, and South Africa may have been middle-income countries for much longer than China and India, but they are not growing out of that status. The real question is, will China and India grow past them or will they become mired in the same middle-income trap?

LOW WAGES OR LOW LABOR COSTS?

The massive increase of manufacturing exports from China and other developing countries is associated in the West with doom scenarios of mass unemployment and destitute workers as international capitalists exploit globalization in association with local elites in developing countries. These developing country elites supposedly use liberalization in the economic realm for imposing political discipline and chronic poverty on their local masses. This exploitation is supposedly made possible by the adoption of authoritarian structures and methods of government even if some appearances of democracy are maintained (as in the case of India). In such a scenario, the challenge of low-cost offshore manufacturing appears so dangerous that there must be no possibility for Western high-wage economies to maintain their competitiveness.

And yet manufacturing output and exports have been relatively stable in developed countries throughout the period of China's rise, and service industries have flourished. The United States, arguably the country most open to Chinese exports and the country that has seen the most of its low-wage manufacturing off-shored, has seen a doubling of its real GDP per capita since the beginning of China's opening to the world. Median wages have stagnated in the United States due to rising inequality, not slow growth or an uncompetitive economy. In the mid-2010s, exports reached an all-time high in the United States, measured either in absolute terms or as a percentage of GDP. The United States has made a series of political decisions in recent decades that have led to rapidly rising inequality, but there is no sign that the US economy has become uncompetitive due to low-cost manufacturing in China. Quite the contrary.

We have mentioned the role played by depressed currency valuations in export-led growth in developing countries. The new export competitiveness of developing countries has not been due to low real wages, even if wage costs in international currency in some countries can be as low as 1/20 (or in extreme cases 1/50) of the developed world's wage costs. No working-class family living in a developed country could survive a 95 percent wage reduction in order to stay competitive with workers in poor countries. Yet as every backpacker knows, developing countries are much cheaper to live in (and India is among the cheapest). Purchasing power parity statistics show that the same US dollar buys nearly four times as much when it is converted into Indian rupees and spent in India—and these statistics are based on country-wide consumption patterns, which are heavily biased toward the consumption of the rich. When imported goods (like automobiles) that are bought primarily by the rich are stripped out of the analysis, the cost of living for the poor in India may be as low as one-tenth as in the United States.

Importantly, this low cost of living in India (and to a lesser extent in China) is not due to a lower standard of living. The point is that the same amount of rice, the same number of eggs, the same area of housing, the same haircut, and the same megabytes of internet service all cost less in developing countries. It is true that both prices and quality tend to be higher in richer countries, but even when comparing like for like in quality the prices are much lower in developing countries. As a result, even though labor costs (as expressed in US dollars) are much less in China and India than they are in the United States, real wages—adjusted for the local cost of living—are actually much closer. A Chinese factory worker earning only one-fifth the salary of a US factory worker may live at something like one half the standard of living.

Figure 3 depicts the relative economy-wide costs of consumption goods in the five BRICS countries compared to the United States. Two caveats are in order. First, the true costs of living for most workers are even lower than these economy-wide averages, since the relative prices of goods consumed by the poor tend to be lower than the relative prices of goods consumed by the rich. Second, it should be remembered that the United States itself has the lowest costs of living of any rich country. Keeping these two facts in mind, Figure 3 clearly shows that India has by far the lowest costs of living of any of the BRICSs. Not coincidentally, it is now the fastest-growing, in terms of both exports and its overall economy. China tied India for very low costs until 2007. After that point its costs began the steep rise that has been associated with its declining international competitiveness and slowing economic growth.

Brazil, by contrast, has consistently had the highest domestic prices (i.e., a relatively overvalued exchange rate), which peaked in the mid-1990s and are once again at historic highs. The Brazilian *real* doubled in relative value between the early 2000s (when Brazil was growing rapidly) and the early 2010s (when growth stalled). Had Brazil channeled the upward pressure on the *real* after 2002 into the accumulation of foreign exchange reserves, it might now have a competitive, growing economy buttressed by massive foreign exchange reserves. Instead it is suffering from a deep recession

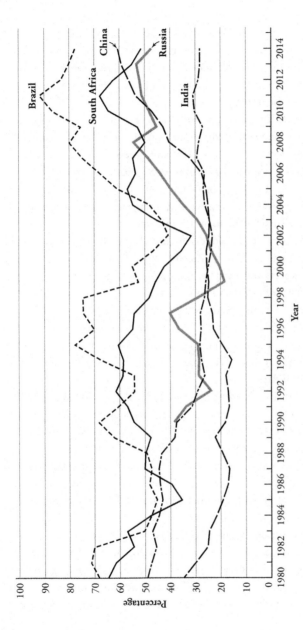

FIGURE 3. Time series of the international US dollar exchange values of the BRICS currencies relative to their domestic purchasing power, 1980–2014.

Source: Authors' calculations based on data from the Penn World Table v.9.0 database.

and facing national bankruptcy. The decade-long run-up in the exchange rate of the *real* may have been very welcome among Brazilians who buy imported goods and like to travel abroad, but it did little to improve the real incomes of ordinary Brazilians who mainly consume in the local market.

Along with Russia and South Africa, Brazil has high (and in Brazil's case, increasing) shares of raw materials in its exports. According to data from the World Bank, the share of raw materials in Brazilian exports rose from 26.8 percent in 2005 to 42.0 percent in 2015. In Russia the proportion fell slightly, from 39.0 to 34.3 percent, but only because of dramatically falling prices for Russian oil. Russia's true focus on mineral exports is even higher, but refined petroleum products are not classified as raw materials in international trade statistics. In South Africa the rise in raw materials exports was modest, from 23.2 to 25.9 percent. By contrast, the share of raw materials exports in China declined over the same period from an already low 9.6 percent to 1.7 percent, while in India it fell from 9.0 to 8.3 percent. Manufactured goods now make up 69.0 percent of India's exports and 94.4 percent of China's, compared to just 36.3 percent in Brazil, 20.4 in Russia, and 47.6 in South Africa.

The key to interpreting these patterns is that exchange rates (and by extension, domestic prices and costs of living) have little impact on raw material exports. In fact, overvalued currencies allow governments to extract rents on raw materials exports, which in developing country settings usually put foreign exchange earnings directly into government hands. In the case of successful exports of manufactures (China and India), the decisive rents to be mobilized come from a surplus of agricultural production. External rents from raw materials could just as easily be used for a policy of devaluation in support of low-cost manufacturing, but they rarely are. The prevailing international advice that growth depends primarily on attracting foreign investment makes such a solution politically difficult, and the use of government resource rents to promote mass consumption can appear wasteful. But appearances can be deceiving.

The empirical evidence strongly suggests that mass consumption is itself the most important driver of foreign investment. More importantly, it leads to capitalist technological progress, which is oriented to decreasing the unit costs of production of goods. Under these conditions, the use of external rents to overcome marginality in living standards of the poor is a sensible strategy. Where direct subsidies are politically infeasible, ambitious infrastructure investment projects (like China's post-2008 railway boom) that create jobs and thus tighten labor markets can be appropriate. But none of the three BRICSs raw materials exporters has used its resource rents in this way. They have instead channeled their resource rents into inflated exchange rates and thus (indirectly) into subsidizing the consumption of the already-rich, who are disproportionately the ones who consume imported and overseas goods and services.

The limits to a strategy of relying on devaluation below purchasing power parity show that the scenario of a permanent underselling of the more advanced economies is unlikely. With export success, exchange rates eventually rise toward parity. But in the meantime, with increasing exports in relatively labor-intensive production processes, structural unemployment is slowly absorbed because private enterprises want to exploit the available cheap labor. This does not mean that labor has to remain cheap. When more and more labor is drawn into the export sector, a scarcity of labor will emerge. China demonstrates that even a highly repressive political system is unable to keep labor from organizing itself and fighting for better salaries and working conditions, including safety in the workplace. Mainland China is here following in the footsteps of Japan, South Korea, and Taiwan. The Chinese leadership may consider its monopoly on decision making as decisive for maintaining political stability, but it has also shown that it understands the necessity to reach compromises with emerging social forces even at the price of reducing the power of its own local representatives. Concessions on wages are, after all, politically easier than concessions on human rights.

Once developing countries approach high levels of employment, the usual mechanisms of capitalist economies begin to be triggered: workers in different branches tend to converge to average wages, which differ mainly according to the cost of education, desirability, and the scarcity of skills. Lower-income groups come to perceive their economic situations as relatively similar, leading to a tendency toward convergence in political action that fosters the creation of broad social coalitions. The continued devaluation of the currency substantially below purchasing power parity becomes increasingly difficult as additional demand for labor from export production allows labor to increase its wages beyond average productivity increases, a process called "imported inflation." Germany in the late 1950s was characterized by such imported inflation and had to accept the appreciation of its exchange rate relative to the US dollar despite massive resistance from German industry. There is no lasting strategy of development with an undervalued currency beyond the initial stage. Korea and Taiwan are good examples of this, as they had to make concessions to their working classes despite rather repressive political systems in the early 1980s.

Perhaps counterintuitively, these struggles are an important part of the transition to capitalism and the development of a high-wage, high-productivity economy. In the early stages of growth, undervalued currencies serve to keep real wages high at the same time as they keep the actual costs of labor low (in foreign currency terms). But a currency can't remain undervalued forever. As the currency rises toward parity with the country's development, other mechanisms must take over the institutional burden of maintaining positive momentum in real wage growth. The more working people are able to negotiate the price of their labor time, the more flexible an export-oriented economy will become in reacting to increasing demands by enabling the growth of mass consumption-oriented industries. Previously export-oriented industries will diversify into local technology production for mass consumption industries. The more export-oriented economies accept flexibility in their class struggles, the shorter the transition period before they become developed capitalist economies with empowered, high-wage workforces.

EXPORT-ORIENTED GROWTH AND THE UPGRADING OF THE PRODUCTION MIX

Export-oriented growth may start with the manufacturing of simple consumer goods like textiles, clothing, shoes, and toys, but the new exporters of manufactured goods rapidly move away from these early patterns. Critics of export-oriented growth have often focused on the initial specialization in light manufacturing without realizing that this is only a step (and a short one at that) on the road to a more diversified economy. Keynesian growth theory, derived from the insights of the English economist John Maynard Keynes, can be used to understand the trajectory of technical upgrading historically observed among the Asian tiger newly industrialized countries and more recently in China. Two branches of production are of particular interest.

Let us look first at machinery and transport equipment, which also includes automobile production. These are traditional high-technology industries which were important for Germany, Japan, and the United States in their own industrial transformations. Data from the United Nations Conference on Trade and Development (UNCTAD) show that exports in this branch of production expanded at double the rate of all manufacturing exports in China and in India between 1995 and 2012 (up 22% per annum in China and 18% in India, with both figures accelerating toward the end of the period). For the whole period, 48 percent of the increase in Chinese exports was due to increased exports of machinery and transport equipment. Although the other BRICSs show appreciable rates of growth in this branch, their rates of growth were all less than 10 percent per annum, or less than the average rate of the rest of the developing world (between 1995 and 2012, 11.7% per annum). In 2006 China overtook Germany in the value of machinery and transport equipment exports.

But as important as heavy machinery may be, the world's mental image of the BRICS countries climbing the ladder of technical development is formed by the rise of China in the field of electronics. Total exports of electronics products, including their parts, increased in China by 20.9 percent per annum between 1995 and 2012 from an already high share in Chinese exports at the start of the period, according to UNCTAD data. Electronics products (including parts and components) now constitute 34 percent of China's exports. India's exports of electronics increased by 15.7 percent per annum between 1995 and 2012, roughly in line with overall exports, though this rate of growth has accelerated in the last ten years to 24 percent. China's exports in electronics goods are now eighty-five times those of India. Catch-up in the new high-technology branch of electronics has not occurred in the BRICSs as a group. It has happened mainly in China—and is now starting to happen in India. In all other BRICSs excluding China and India, not only do raw materials remain an important focus of exports but the traditional light-industrial export industries remain important as well.

Whereas China (and to a much lesser extent India) has been able to supplement and supplant these traditional industries with new exports in areas like transportation equipment and electronics, the other three BRICSs rely much more on raw materials and resource-intensive industries. Their share of low-skill and "medium-skill technology-intensive" industries is high at around 60 to 80 percent. In China and India the equivalent figure is closer to one-third. Electronics goods of any level of technical sophistication are nearly absent in the export increases of Brazil, South Africa, and

Russia to developed countries. Medium and low technology is at the center of their increases in manufactured exports to developing countries with electronic goods of any level of sophistication being virtually absent also here. The export miracle of China consists in entry into electronic high-tech products which are produced with high-import content, not in its exports of low- or medium-technology products.

There is therefore no danger of the BRICSs as a group overtaking the developed countries, but the fact that China was able to become competitive in new high technologies requires an explanation. The transformative role of the Chinese export sector, especially exports to the developed countries, results from the increasing competitiveness of China in new technologies (i.e., electronics). These new technologies are accessible to all countries of the Global South, but among the BRICSs only China has really benefited. A provocative observation is the fact that China and the countries which preceded it in specialization in electronics did not show major increases in the export of medium-level technology. They seem to have jumped from low-technology light manufacturing exports straight to high-technology electronics exports—a leap that Vietnam seems to be making right now. This appears to be in contradiction with standard theories on stable hierarchies in international specialization and the inevitability of specialization by comparative advantage that is expected to accompany opening to the world market.

By contrast, Keynesian and endogenous growth theory argue that growth depends not only (or even primarily) on the accumulation of physical capital but much more so on the development of human capital—ultimately, learning (often learning-by-doing). The inevitable result of increasing human capital is convergence in GDP per capita. In this view, the comparative advantage of a relatively backward economy does not lie in the leading technologies of the past, where the productivity lag is high due to an absence of learning-by-doing in the backward economy. Somewhat counterintuitively, once

human capital is taken into account the comparative advantage of
the backward economies is greatest in the leading technologies of the
future, where there is a more level playing field because no country
has yet developed the requisite skills to succeed.

An established leading economy will probably be superior to a
backward economy even when a new leading technology emerges.
The established leading economy will not, however, be able to
transfer 100 percent of its productivity advantage into the new
leading branch. Both developed economies and catch-up economies are in the same situation of having no accumulated learning-
by-doing in new leading technologies, but developed economies
do have massive amounts of human capital already committed to
older branches of production that cannot be entirely transferred
to the new leading branch. Consequently, developed countries
have a comparative advantage in old, established leading branches
while developing countries have a comparative advantage in newly
emerging leading branches. Germany overtook Britain at the end
of the nineteenth century not because Germany was superior in
electrical or chemical products, but because it was so much infe-
rior in the traditional well-earning high-technology branch of that
time, high-quality textiles.

Therefore the rise of parts of the Global South (particularly
China) in new industries is not a symptom of the decay of the
West but is instead the normal result of the operation of capitalism. The problem is not whether the West is existentially chal-
lenged by the rise of the emerging countries, but whether this rise
is sufficiently fast to keep the West from triggering off an under-
consumption crisis. Rising inequality in nearly all developed
countries threatens the mass character of consumption on which
capitalism depends for its very existence as an economic system.
The best thing the West could do to stave off a rising China would
be to increase the wages of its own workers, who do not by and
large compete directly with Chinese ones. The next best thing
might be for developed countries to promote mass consumption
in China itself.

Interestingly, the most profitable branch of industry for Western companies operating in China is transportation equipment. This "old" leading industry is one where Western companies have the greatest accumulated knowledge of learning-by-doing. China has become both the most important export market for North American and European car companies and at the same time the most important overseas production market. India is following fast behind. China and India may be emerging as leading producers in the new industrial branches of electronics hardware and software, but they are also emerging as crucial markets in the old (but still highly profitable) industrial branch of automobile manufacturing. China could break out of (and India could attain) middle-income status through continued upgrading in new branches of production, but this is only possible if global consumer markets continue to grow. The maintenance of the global capitalist system is beyond the control of BRICS governments, even one so powerful as China. But if declining mass incomes in the developed West make it impossible for China to export its way to full development, it will have to put even more resources into increasing incomes within China itself.

THE CONTRIBUTION OF INTERNATIONAL CAPITAL

The growth of the stock of foreign direct investment (FDI) in the BRICSs appears at first glance to be tremendous, increasing by 15.7 percent per annum between 1995 and 2012. Most of the net increase since 2003, however, has been due to Russia, India, and Brazil. The rate of increase of foreign direct investment stock in China was just 5.8 percent per annum between 2003 and 2012, lower than the average both of the BRICSs and of developing countries as a whole. In fact, the amount of foreign direct investment in the three weaker-performing BRICSs increased from 50 percent of the amount invested in China in 1995 to 52 percent in 2003, and 103 percent in 2012. Yet China remains the undisputed champion exporter among the BRICS countries. This makes clear the fact that there is no direct relation between openness to FDI and export performance.

Whereas the three poorer-performing BRICSs have stocks of foreign direct investment that are close to the developing country average of 30 to 40 percent of GDP, the two better-performing BRICSs, China and India, have much lower stocks. China's stock of foreign direct investment constitutes around 10 percent of GDP (a level it has maintained since 2003), while India has stabilized at around this value since 2010. This does not contradict the idea that openness to international cooperation is important for catching up, but it does qualify the statement: openness may be helpful if it is usefully instrumentalized by the strategy applied by the catching-up economy. Investment openness is not in itself an automatic motor of rapid industrialization.

Comparable international statistics are not available on the branch structure of FDI in different countries, but data are available for FDI country of origin. These data suggest that China has a relatively high share of FDIs coming from industrial partners. Leaving aside tax havens like the British Virgin Islands, five out of the six top sources of FDI into China are neighboring Asian jurisdictions: Japan, Taiwan, South Korea, Singapore, and Hong Kong. The sixth is the United States. All of these are leading countries in production networks that extend across Pacific borders into China. By contrast, most of the European Union FDI stock in Brazil (56%) has its origins in Luxembourg and the Netherlands. These investments are highly unlikely to represent Brazilian participation in high-technology manufacturing value chains along which it could climb to higher levels of productivity.

Another indicator of the character of a country's integration into the global economy is the share of transnational enterprises in export production. In the initial phase of China's export boom, FDI played an important role. It raised its share in total exports in some of the more innovative branches like electronics to almost 50 percent. Hong Kong investors were particularly important in shifting production to neighboring Guangdong province in the Pearl River Delta, while Taiwanese investors operated indirectly in Guangdong (via Hong Kong) and directly in the Yangtze River Delta. South Korean and Japanese investors have been more important in the heavy industries of northern China, particularly automobile production, which also attracted early joint venture partners from Germany and the United States.

The foreign shares in these industries tend to decline over time. German car manufacturers have already lost market share in the Chinese domestic market, and transnational enterprises continue to lose market share in Chinese electronics exports. In the case of major investment goods, like numerically controlled machine tools, Chinese producers were able to enlarge their shares by specializing on the lower complexity end of these products. Against the argument that this demonstrates further dependence of Chinese producers on foreign technology, it can be argued that the rapid expansion of the Chinese mass markets together with a specialization on simple products has allowed China to enter the machine-producing branch from the lower end. Chinese domestic firms' initial focus on the low end of the market is allowing them to acquire the learning-by–doing experience necessary for assimilating more advanced technologies and to engage in successful reverse engineering.

Learning acquired in successful specialization on the lower end can be upgraded by cooperating with transnational enterprises and ultimately moving to external markets. The acquisition of skills by specializing on the lower end locally appears to be a condition for successful upgrading via the world market. Any technologically backward economy has additional costs in moving to higher levels of technology in comparison to more advanced economies. Companies from economically backward countries can avail themselves of cheaper labor costs, especially cheaper costs of trained and educated labor. Therefore governments engage in comprehensive education, as China does but also India, and to a lesser degree Russia, Brazil, and South Africa. The most recent development consists, however, in moving abroad. Buying companies in technically more advanced countries is an important mechanism for further employee training and management learning-by-doing.

The knowledge base of local companies can be further enhanced by promotional measures financed from government spending, often acquired in effect by the government's capacity to tax high-earning export industries, which can sell to developed markets already at relatively high prices in relation to local costs. Singapore financed the upgrading of its workforce in the early 1980s by taxing low-skill exports and raising minimum wages by 20 percent per year for three years in a row. When cooperation between local companies and transnational companies is successful, the opposition between cost-driven and market-driven FDI disappears. In the 1980s China attracted high levels of cost-driven FDI from companies in other Asian countries that were attracted by low wages, at the same time as it attracted high levels of market-driven FDI from companies in developed countries that wanted to produce inside China for the expanding Chinese market. Rising real wages in local currency terms that were still low by international standards made this possible. Moreover, the undervalued but (as a result) consistently rising currency almost ensured that long-term FDI would generate a profit.

This pattern resembles in some ways the investment offensives which had taken place in Latin America during the period of import substituting industrialization in the middle of the twentieth century. The key obstacles to Latin America's industrialization were stagnant mass incomes and overvalued exchange rates. In contrast, China's rising incomes and undervalued exchange rate allowed advanced investors to earn immediate profits while giving Chinese enterprises the opportunity to benefit from technically more advanced foreign companies. The Chinese instrumentalization of foreign technologies through demonstration effects was denounced in international commentary as China copying Western technologies, but Western companies profited (and continue to profit) handsomely from their operations in China—or they wouldn't be there. Western companies clearly calculate that the immediate economic benefits of operating in China outweigh the long-term threat posed by their Chinese partners.

Using their massive internal market as the basis for increasing sales, Chinese enterprises naturally have a comparative advantage in selling products to less-advanced countries. This was observed as early as the 1980s. By the mid-2000s Chinese enterprises were able to start competing in the markets of developed countries, though for now they still lag in most industries. This trajectory is very similar to that followed by (for example) the South Korean auto industry, which followed the Japanese auto industry in conquering markets first in developing countries and later in developed ones. All of these cases have depended on the initial development of an internal mass market, which allowed the development of locally produced investment goods that met the low-quality requirements of local low-income customers. Many countries look to Africa, Southeast Asia, Latin America, and the Middle East for low-income customers for (initially) low-quality products, but India and China can still find these customers within their own borders.

With the reliance of the BRICSs on markets for relatively simple goods, the monopolistic control of high technology by the developed-country suppliers of technology has been less important. The leading branches for this kind of catching-up development do not require the typical forms of control of technical knowledge by monopoly described in the FDI-based development theory of Stephen Hymer. Today's postmodern global value chains are demand driven and essentially based on control of marketing channels, not supply driven and based on the control of technology. The developmentalist rhetoric of the Global South against the new international division of labor with high-technology production centered in the developed countries must therefore be taken with a grain of salt. The actual drive of the Global South for a new international division of labor can be interpreted as a check on the tendencies to oligopoly immanent in the centralization of capitalism around developed-country brands. In many cases the most advanced technology as such is increasingly to be found in the Global South, where new branches of production are concentrated.

Some caveats are, however, necessary. The expansion of emerging economies abroad (first to other less-developed countries, later to developed ones) is not triggered only by new or high-technology companies that are keen to increase the size of their markets. It also results from simple capital flight. Capital exports show an extreme importance of financial offshore centers. One-fourth of the stock of the Indian foreign capital is in the financial center of Mauritius, and if Singapore is included then the proportion in tax havens increases to one-third. One-fifth of South African external capital and two-thirds of Russian is in financial centers like Cyprus, Luxembourg, and the Virgin Islands. The external capital of the BRICS countries is apparently invested to a large percentage in financial (or at least opaque) speculation, not in production.

The highly competitive branches of industry that can be taxed by home governments in developing countries often rely on state support when they seek to expand internationally. This automatically triggers tendencies for increasing inequality in the distribution of income, especially as long as labor is disempowered because of mass unemployment. Thus Brazil, Russia, and South Africa long predate China and India in the internationalization of their capital investments, not because their industries are more advanced but because their labor is less empowered. These tendencies toward capital flight are greatly supported by the general ideological order created by the leading capitalist developed economies like the United States and the United Kingdom, which act as safe harbors for deposed elites of the South (and their money) when they fall from political favor.

Given an international order that is highly charitable to capital flight, it is crucial for developing countries to develop their domestic economies and international competitiveness on the basis of their own social and political structures. Whether China, the BRICSs, and the rest of the Global South will catch up to the developed world or remain mired in the middle-income trap will therefore depend not only on economic mechanisms but on the robustness of their own policy environments. The policies that are necessary for catch-up depend only on the short-term profit motivation of technologically advanced companies based in developed countries, and the long-term commitment of the governments of developing countries to using rents productively rather than squander them. Advanced companies can be safely relied on to pursue profits. Ultimately, then, the success of developing countries depends on the outcomes of their internal class struggles over the allocation of rents in their own economies.

CONCLUSION

The middle-income trap is just that: a trap. It is not an inevitable destiny or a foregone conclusion. It is a trap that can be avoided or, once sprung, escaped.

Brazil seems caught in the middle-income trap by an overvalued currency and impending austerity measures. Over the last eighty years there have been many false dawns in Brazil. Russia wasted the potential to use the rents from its oil boom to finance improvements in the rest of the economy. Now it is similarly wasting the opportunity to use its depressed exchange rate to do the same. India is still relatively poor and may have the opportunity to avoid the middle-income trap entirely, but to do so it will have to make much more strenuous efforts to raise employment and income. South Africa, like Brazil, has been caught in the middle-income trap for generations. The end of apartheid and the transition to democracy in 1994 raised hopes of a new start, but the ANC government has repeatedly failed to live up to expectations.

China has long seemed the developing world's best bet to avoid the middle-income trap. It raised mass incomes spectacularly between 1980 and 2015, accounting for nearly all of the global reduction in poverty over that period. It retained a relatively weak currency until 2007, building up a currency reserve of four trillion dollars in the process. All that changed after the global financial crisis. China navigated the crisis itself brilliantly, unleashing a fiscal stimulus similar in size to that of the United States but relatively speaking roughly twice the size, adjusted for the size of the economy at the time. But left with the bill for all that spending, the new administration that took office in 2013 seems to have chosen austerity over growth. It has embraced a rhetoric about a "new normal" of slower growth and prepared the political ground for mass layoffs in government-owned firms. It has also reversed China's historical weak-Yuan policy, spending some one trillion dollars in a vain effort to prop up the value of the Yuan. In short, China's political elite is preparing to lock in the gains of the last thirty-five years rather than double-down on the path to growth.

Thus the prospects seem slim that any of the five BRICS countries will escape the middle-income trap, though that judgment may be premature in the case of India. The reasons for this are not primarily economic. They are political. In all five countries entrenched elites seem likely to succeed in putting their own interests (low wages coupled with high currency valuations and capital mobility) above those of the mass of working people. The Asian tigers that previously escaped the middle-income trap had very different social structures from the five BRICSs. Japan eviscerated its prewar elite under US occupation, while South Korea and Taiwan did the same to their inherited pro-Japanese elites when they became independent of Japan. Singapore was a beleaguered refugee state populated by Straits Chinese from across Southeast Asia. None of these Asian tigers were ordinary countries ruled by long-entrenched elites. They were all countries caught up in rapid social structural change during their periods of most rapid growth. China may have opened its economy to the private sector, but contemporary China is ruled by the very children and grandchildren of the Communist Party officials who seized power in 1949.

Could the BRICSs escape the middle-income trap? Certainly yes. The necessary policies are on the table. But they are unlikely to be taken up so long as the countries' political systems continue to be controlled by a small number of families with long-term interests in keeping things as they are.

THE BRICS CHALLENGE

Could the growth process in the BRICSs be sustainable and continue to be sustainably high enough to lift them out of middle-income status? The government-to-business relations of state support to private enterprise that prevail in the BRICS countries provide possibilities for accelerated accumulation, increasing technical skills, and enhanced international competitiveness, but they may equally lead to spoon feeding, monopoly, and restrictions on growth. Internal power relations that sometimes favor the poor can create negotiating power for workers in employment, but they can also generate large rents in favor of special interest groups. Integration into the world economy can provide jobs, but it can also generate rents for some branches and particular companies. Many of the mechanisms that we have identified in this book have contributed to inequality and privilege, corruption and waste, even if they also had the effect of empowering labor via employment.

Specialization in labor-intensive products, with increasing competitiveness in more complex products, pushes employment higher because of the high price elasticity of these products (which rewards economies of scale since lower prices generate more and more demand). In relatively open economies this improves international competitiveness as well. The high-income elasticity of demand for these products in the dynamically catching-up economies (and especially in the leading industrialized countries) means that the burden of undervalued currencies falls mainly on those who can most afford it, while the benefits of expanded production accrue mainly to the poor workers who are in the greatest need.

This is the fundamental linkage that explains why some of the BRICS countries have succeeded better than others. The crucial

policy goal is not to ensure that incomes are high through high
export earnings, but that employment is high through high export
volumes. Increasing employment through increasing exports may
trigger internal market expansion provided that labor has the
resources and resourcefulness to ensure its own well-being,
whether that self-sufficiency comes from entitlement to land, as in
China, or entitlement to government support, as in Brazil, India,
and (to an increasing extent) South Africa. The more such entitle-
ments exist—even if at low levels—the more increasing employment in export sectors for low-skilled labor will trigger rising
internal demand with additional employment for internal market-
oriented industries.

But such processes create powerful counterforces that push in
the opposite direction. As these countries are characterized by
widespread underemployment and rent-collecting arrangements
for the privileged, overall economic growth may not lead to commensurate increases in employment levels. This is the key problem
in Russia, which failed to use a decade of high oil rents from 2004
to 2014 to develop the rest of its economy. Aside from political
pressure for more generous pensions, the mass of the population
was unable to benefit from high oil prices because workers were
not sufficiently empowered to take on the political power of the
corrupt ruling elites, who were able to use political power to capture most of the benefits. The high levels of inequality in the
BRICSs, especially the high incomes of the very rich, are ultimately if indirectly the result of a failure of export-oriented and
mass consumption industries to generate enough employment to
make labor scarce.

The high amounts of capital held in offshore financial centers,
often estimated at around twenty trillion dollars, are indirectly the
result of market failures, as possibilities for productive investment
are limited due to a lack of mass demand. Producers are not forced
to lower prices and increase wages when productivity and employment increase, as they would be expected to do in a truly capitalist

economy. Instead they face incentives to internalize and hoard their gains. This problem is not limited to developing countries: America's leading technology companies unproductively hold hundreds of billions of dollars in offshore tax havens. But the problem is most acutely felt in developing countries, where employment levels are low and capital is scarce. Whether the expansion of mass markets will emerge victorious over political rent seeking in those countries that are trying to avoid or escape the middle-income trap depends on the speed with which employment and production can be expanded. The outcome of each country's internal social struggles will play a major part in the decision. But the global intellectual environment matters too. Local elites pay close attention to the signals that come from powerful international organizations, universities, and governments.

The Western fear of the BRICSs as some kind of antisystemic project is entirely unwarranted: the rise of the BRICSs is just the most recent chapter in the much larger story of the expansion of capitalism. The international search for cheap labor is a good thing (from the perspective of the capitalist system as a whole) and—contrary to popular perceptions—it doesn't undermine wages in already developed countries. The problem of low wages in the United States is an entirely political phenomenon, which should be obvious from the fact that the lowest wages are in the kinds of consumer service industries (retailing and fast food) that are not subject to international competition. Nor is the expansion of high-technology production in the BRICSs a threat to the West's own industries. The BRICSs are most successful where they enjoy a comparative advantage, that is in branches of production that are not already well developed in the West.

The international search for cheap labor is ultimately salutary because it is ultimately transitory if it is allowed to run its course. It leads to fully capitalist economies with scarcity of labor if the process is not held up by market failure. Seen from this standpoint, persistently low wages are not a sign of market success but a sign that capitalism is not functioning properly. In the late nineteenth century, Germany did not overtake the United Kingdom because of its low wages. Germany overtook Britain despite its high wages, which led to an expanding internal market. German companies did not compete on the basis of low prices in well-established industries where Britain already had a massive lead; they competed on their comparative (though not absolute) advantage in newly emerging branches of production with new technologies. But the success of Germany did not lead to the demise of the United Kingdom. Britain today has roughly the same GDP per capita as Germany, even if both fall well short of the United States.

Among the BRICSs, those that are most successful have expanded their internal markets and accepted increasing mass incomes. Incomes have risen so much in China that there is now a small but highly visible trend of "reshoring" jobs from China to the United States. The use of technology is spreading and production processes that would have remained labor intensive if labor had remained cheap are starting to be mechanized. The Chinese case also demonstrates that even undemocratic governments cannot block rising mass incomes when labor becomes scarce. This confirms the experience of pre-1914 Germany, where despite a relatively authoritarian political system, big business could not block rising real wages when labor became scarce. In the Nordic countries, which always had more egalitarian income distributions, industrialization occurred in technically advanced ways right from the very beginning. If the BRICSs succeed in breaking out of the middle-income trap, they will become valued partners in the global capitalist system, just as Germany and the Nordic countries are today.

By contrast, those southern and eastern European countries that had high levels of inequality and low levels of employment in the nineteenth century did not experience broad-based technological innovation, despite becoming industrialized. The east-central European areas that became the countries of Poland,

Hungary, Czech Republic, and Slovakia were heavily industrialized in the late nineteenth and early twentieth centuries, but their
governments (originally German, Austrian, and Russian, then
after 1918 independent) redirected agricultural rents toward elite
landowners rather than ordinary workers. The same was true in
Prussia, the historical core of the modern German state, which
became a social backwater of the united Germany and was ultimately stripped from Germany in the aftermath of the world
wars. The failure to generate mass prosperity in these eastern
European territories resulted from a failure to implement fully
capitalist social relations, not from a capitalist exploitation of
cheap labor. Similar failures plague eastern Europe even today. It
is no coincidence that the best-performing economy in eastern
Europe belongs to the country (Poland) that retained its own
weak currency rather than joining the overvalued euro.

The question of the middle-income trap is therefore not new.
But the lessons of history have not been well learned. Despite the
existence of many historical examples from Europe in the nineteenth century and Asia in the twentieth, the importance of rising
mass incomes as a condition for the transition to capitalism is
rarely mentioned. Western-trained economists too often focus on
circuitous supply-side arguments instead of direct demand-side
ones. So while the IMF and other intergovernmental organizations
now recognize the empirical link between high inequality and low
growth, they avoid the obvious conclusion that the problem posed
by high inequality is that it is usually associated with low wages.
China has become very unequal, but it has also experienced dramatic increases in ordinary people's wages. As a result, Chinese
companies invest heavily in developing mass production technologies, which are the very basis of capitalist accumulation. High
inequality is a challenge for China, but not for the supply-side
reasons given by the IMF (e.g., that high inequality harms healthcare and education systems and undermines political support for
neoliberal policies). High inequality is a challenge for China
because it limits demand by limiting the incomes of the poor.

In the absence of a strong pressure from below, the main challenge facing the BRICS countries is that economic growth will serve and empower the rent-seeking classes of the new rich before the mass of the population comes to be empowered through labor scarcity. This is now happening in China as the ruling Communist Party asks its population to accept the "new normal" of slower growth rather than implement policies that might compromise the political-economic power of the economic elite—which is drawn almost entirely from the families of the ruling Communist Party elite. Pressures from the new rich to put a lid on the market pressures unleashed by capitalism are prevailing in China despite initially strong sociocultural and ideological norms in favor of egalitarianism and meritocracy. The great proponents of a truly competitive capitalism in China today are not the country's billionaires (who are overwhelmingly concentrated in state-related industries) but the workers of the eastern provinces of the country, where labor has already become scarce and has started to self-organize against the most egregious manifestations of inequality and exploitation.

CONVERGENCE TO WHAT?

If the BRICSs do not manage to avoid (China and India) or escape (Brazil, Russia, South Africa) the middle-income trap, they won't be the only countries stuck at middle income levels. None of the countries of Latin America has ever converged to high-income status. The richest among them, Chile and Uruguay, are still much poorer than Greece, Spain, Portugal, and other countries on the European periphery. A quarter century after their liberation from Soviet occupation, the countries of east-central Europe have failed to make much progress in terms of overall GDP per capita. And the countries of the Middle East have perennially failed to use their natural resource rents to finance the transition to full employment and high wages. It's not just the BRICSs that are caught in the middle-income trap. Nearly everyone is.

Given that the world as a whole has a GDP per capita of around $10,000 per year, one might wonder why middle income should be considered a trap at all. Seen from a global perspective, middle-income status is in many ways simply ordinary, the world average level of economic success. Nonetheless, a common plea made by people who live in middle-income countries is that they wish they could live in a "normal" country: a country where there is no corruption, where government is responsive, and where all people can earn a decent standard of living. Such utopias may not be common in today's world, but they are nonetheless "normal"— that is, the kinds of countries that people consider socially acceptable for themselves and their families. The BRICSs may be typical, but North America, Western Europe, and (more recently) East Asia are "normal."

But the very characteristics that have made the developed countries seem normal in the eyes of the rest of the world may now be under threat. They are not threatened by the rise of the BRICSs; development is not a zero-sum game. Increased manufacturing productivity in China has dramatically improved well-being in the rest of the world, not undermined it, since it has driven down the cost of living without doing anything to reduce productivity elsewhere. Quite the contrary: productivity improvements in China have in effect produced rents that can be (and in some cases have been) used to subsidize workers in other countries. The good things that people enjoy in the developed West are not threatened by the BRICSs. They are threatened from within.

Wage stagnation has become a general feature of the developed world, starting first in the United States in the 1980s, then spreading to Japan in the 1990s and to Western Europe in the 2000s. Labor is becoming increasingly disempowered. The US economy has effectively deunionized since the 1970s. Japanese job-for-life practices have largely disappeared. German wage coordination now in effect coordinates wage cuts instead of wage increases. Labor flexibility has become the zeitgeist of the twenty-first

century. The result is that productivity gains are outstripping production increases due to low wages (and consequent low demand),
leading to chronic underemployment. Nearly all of the processes
that have been highlighted in this book as steps for climbing the
ladder of development are now operating in reverse in the world's
most developed countries. Instead of wondering if the BRICSs
will escape the middle-income trap, we should perhaps be worrying that the West will fall into it.

The middle-income trap is, in the final analysis, a political trap,
not an economic one. It is a political trap that the economy falls
into when capitalism is not comprehensively applied as a system
for organizing a country's economy. By "capitalism" we mean simply "an economy based on production for profit"—and although
leading firms in today's developed countries may be highly profitable, that profit is increasingly based on tax arbitrage, political
concessions, the immiseration of labor, and monopoly power. In a
word, it is not profit at all, but rent. As income inequality has
risen over the last few decades, Western governments have become
increasingly beholden to their wealthiest citizens and largest companies, leading ordinary people to feel alienated, disaffected, and
disenfranchised. It's not just the developing world where people
are dissatisfied with their unresponsive governments. It's the
developed world too.

To the extent that Western governments pursue BRICS-like
economic policies, transforming their countries from capitalist
economies based on the profit motive back into precapitalist countries that reward on rent-seeking behavior, we would expect them
to converge down to middle-income status. This process may occur
so slowly that it goes unnoticed until it is too late. Consider that
the average real per capita growth of the US economy over the last
150 years has been around 2 percent per year. A policy that compromises potential economic growth by half, reducing long-term
trend growth from 2 to 1 percent, would hardly be noticed for a
quarter century or more. It may be happening already: the fifteen

years from 2000 to 2015 have been the slowest-growth period in
American history, with growth averaging slightly less than 1 percent per year. Is this the beginning of a long-term convergence to
middle-income status? It is impossible to say for sure. But the possibility is surely provocative—and worrying.

FINAL THOUGHTS

The BRICS economies are very diverse, reflecting the full diversity
of the Global South. They serve as a good symbol for the Global
South because they are a highly visible but still broadly representative sample of challenges and opportunities that exist throughout
the less developed countries of the world. Like other developing
countries, the BRICSs participate to different degrees in a much
larger global process of industrial competition through currency
devaluation in economies that have relatively low levels of formal
paid employment. Few developing countries have fully valued currencies, and those that do (like Brazil) face stagnation. But currency devaluation is not enough. It must be combined with policies
that promote full employment, higher wages, and the empowerment of labor. The green revolution of the 1960s and 1970s made it
possible for nearly all countries to feed themselves. As a result,
nearly all countries have more workers than they have to employ in
agriculture. The question is, what will they do with them?

Two conclusions seem obvious. First, those people should be
put to work. It is advisable to promote growth across the Global
South, including in the BRICSs, wherever it is possible to increase
levels of formal paid employment. Furthermore, employment
growth should be promoted in ways that are environmentally sustainable. More capital-intensive production based on well-com-
pensated labor is inherently more environmentally friendly than
the kinds of exploitative low-wage arrangements that well-functioning capitalism makes obsolete. Contrary to popular opinion,
the BRICS countries (most notoriously China) have ruined their

environments through a lack of development, not as a conse-
quence of development. The most polluting industries in these
countries are exactly those that are uncompetitive but favored by
the government (chemicals and steel), not those that are most
closely associated with the developing capitalist market economy.
The further empowerment of labor through full employment and
higher wages would reinforce pressures toward environmental
stewardship, not undermine them.

Second, it is probable that the future world economy will not
resemble the models portrayed in standard neoclassical under-
graduate textbooks. Even when economies are able to make a
rapid transition to full employment, firms are too slow in adjust-
ing to changes in comparative advantages and adopting the most
productive modern technologies. They need, if not a helping
hand, then perhaps a kick in the pants from the state. Only the
state serves (or at least should serve) the interests of the community at large. Government intervention may routinely be required
to manage economic rents, but governments just as routinely
abuse political power to protect sectors and companies considered
(often wrongly) to be economically or politically essential. Thus
governments must be held accountable for ensuring the well-
being of the broad mass of the population through their active
management of market mechanisms. We agree with the dominant
view that markets are crucial for economic development, but we
stress that markets must be used for a purpose, not be presumed
to operate autonomously.

The BRICSs are much more united by their international status
as regional powers based on size, population, and influence than
by their economic position within the Global South. Western fears
about the rise of the BRICSs risk sidetracking global economic
debates into a simplistic discussion about the conflicting priorities
of basically selfish powers that are unable to find common ground
in the cooperative management of the world economy. A better,
alternative understanding of the mechanisms leading to the new

international division of labor shows that the increasing participation of the poor in prosperity would reduce the conflict between leading and lagging economies. The task of convincing elites to adopt policies that foster the development of internal mass markets would be facilitated by a more inclusive approach to international economic management. This would limit the ability of governments to claim that international pressures prevent them from pursuing good policies. The rise of the BRICSs creates a degree of political space that can be used to improve economic governance for the whole world.

The middle-income trap can be overcome if appropriate policies are implemented, policies that create employment through increasing mass consumption. National political elites have the power to implement these policies, and it is imperative that pressure be maintained on them to pursue such a trajectory. Elites certainly follow selfish interests. They nonetheless define their interests on the basis of beliefs about social and economic mechanisms and their perceptions of power relations. They are sensitive not only to political pressures but also to academic debate, especially if it is visibly reflected in the public space. For too long economists have provided intellectual cover for elites to believe that economic growth is achieved through low wages and beggar-thy-workers policies. Higher labor costs are certainly costs of production, but profit is ultimately the result of investment spending, and investment is always a response to increasing mass demand. The promotion of mass consumption triggers additional investment in a virtuous circle that ultimately leads to higher profits for elites as well as rising incomes for the masses.

In the simplest language possible, you can't cut your way to prosperity. You have to grow your way to prosperity. And in economies that have not yet reached their full potential, higher wages and full employment are the keys to growth.

SUGGESTED READINGS

INTRODUCTION

Akamatsu, Kaname. 1962. "A Historical Pattern of Economic Growth in Developing Countries." *The Developing Economies* 1(s1): 3–25.

Cohen, Theodore. 1987. *Remaking Japan: The American Occupation as New Deal*. New York: Free Press.

Heckman, James J. 2005. "The Scientific Model of Causality." *Sociological Methodology* 35: 1–97.

Krugman, Paul. 1994. "The Myth of Asia's Miracle." *Foreign Affairs* 73(6): 62–78.

O'Neill, Jim. 2011. *The Growth Map: Economic Opportunity in the BRICs and Beyond*. London: Penguin.

Summers, Lawrence H. 2016. "The Age of Secular Stagnation." *Foreign Affairs* 95(2): 2–9.

van de Walle, Nicolas. 2016. "Making Sense of the Central African Republic." *Foreign Affairs* 95(1): 190.

CHAPTER 1

Barro, Robert, and Jong-Wha Lee. 2015. *Education Matters: Global Schooling Gains from the 19th to the 21st Century*. Oxford: Oxford University Press.

Bond, Patrick, and Ana Garcia (eds.). 2015. *BRICS: An Anti-capitalist Critique*. Auckland Park: Jacana Media.

Communist Party of China. 1978. "Communique of the Third Plenary Session of the 11th Central Committee of the Communist Party of China." *Peking Review* 21(52): 6–16.

de Coning, Cedric, Thomas Mandrup, and Liselotte Osgaard (eds.). 2015. *The BRICS and Coexistence: An Alternative Vision of World Order*. Oxford: Routledge.

Frank, Andre Gunder. 1966. *The Development of Underdevelopment*. New York: Monthly Review Press.

Goldman, Marshall. 2010. *Petrostate: Putin, Power, and the New Russia*. Oxford: Oxford University Press.

Holmes, Leslie. 2015. *Corruption: A Short Introduction*. Oxford: Oxford University Press.

Kiely, Ray. 2015. *The BRICs, US "Decline" and Global Transformations*. London: Palgrave.

Kohli, Atul. 2012. *Poverty amid Plenty in the New India*. Cambridge: Cambridge University Press.

Kurlantzick, Joshua. 2016. *State Capitalism: How the Return of Statism Is Transforming the World*. Oxford: Oxford University Press.

Maddison, Angus. 2007. *Contours of the World Economy, 1–2030 AD*. Oxford: Oxford University Press.

Reid, Michael. 2014. *Brazil: The Troubled Rise of a Global Power*. New Haven: Yale University Press.

So, Alvin, and Yin-Wah Chu. 2015. *The Global Rise of China*. Cambridge: Polity Press.

Williamson, John (ed.). 1990. *Latin American Adjustment: How Much Has Happened?* Washington: Peterson Institute for International Economics.

CHAPTER 2

Acemoglu, Daron, and James A. Robinson. 2012. *Why Nations Fail: The Origins of Power, Prosperity, and Poverty*. New York: Crown.

Barro, Robert, and Jong-Wha Lee. 2015. *Education Matters: Global Schooling Gains from the 19th to the 21st Century*. Oxford: Oxford University Press.

D'Costa, Anthony P. 2009. "Economic Nationalism in Motion: Steel, Auto, and Software Industries in India." *Review of International Political Economy* 16(4): 620–48.

Melville, Andrei, and Mikhail Mironyuk. 2016. "'Bad Enough Governance': State Capacity and Quality of Institutions in Post-Soviet Autocracies." *Post-Soviet Affairs* 32: 132–51.

Saha, Biswatosh. 2004. "State Support for Industrial R and D in Developing Economies. Telecom Equipment Industry in India and China." *Economic and Political Weekly* 39(35): 3915–25.

Scerri, Mario. 2014. "Modes of Innovation and the National Systems of Innovation of the BRICs Economies." *Science Technology and Innovation Policy Review* 5(2): 20–42.

CHAPTER 3

Barros, Ricardo, Mirela de Carvalho, Samuel Franco, and Rosane Mendoça. 2010. "Markets, the State, and the Dynamics of Inequality in Brazil." In *Declining Inequality in Latin America: A Decade of Progress?*, edited by Luis F. López-Calva and Nora Lustig, 134–74. Washington, D.C.: Brookings Institution Press.

Brandt, Loren, and Eric Thun. 2010. "The Fight for the Middle: Upgrading, Competition, and Industrial Development in China." *World Development* 38(11): 1555–74.

Chandra, Nirmal Kumar. 2009. "China and India: Convergence in Economic Growth and Social Tensions?" *Economic and Political Weekly* 44(4): 41–53.

Egawa, Akio. 2013. *Will Income Inequality Cause a Middle Income Trap in Asia?* Bruegel Working Papers 6. Brussels: Bruegel.

Elsenhans, Hartmut. 1992. *Equality and Development*. Dhaka: Center for Social Studies.

Goodman, David S. G. 2014. *Class in Contemporary China*. Cambridge: Polity Press.

Kharas, Homi, and Harinder Kohli. 2011. "What Is the Middle Income Trap, Why Do Countries Fall into It, and How Can It Be Avoided?" *Global Journal of Emerging Market Economies* 3(3): 281–89.

Lavergne, Rémi Fernand, and Bernadete Beserra. 2016. "The Bolsa Família Program. Replacing Politics with Biopolitics." *Latin American Perspectives* 43(2): 96–115.

Lee, Cheol-Sung. 2012. "Associational Networks and Welfare States in Argentina, Brazil, South-Korea, and Taiwan." *World Politics* 64(3): 507–54.

Rodrik, Dani. 2016. "Premature Deindustrialization." *Journal of Economic Growth* 21(1): 1–33.

CHAPTER 4

Baumann, Renato. 2013. "Brazilian, Chinese, and Indian Exports: Is the Regional Market Really a Source of Learning?" *Brazilian Journal of Political Economy* 33(1): 102–19.

Elsenhans, Hartmut. 2002. "Macroeconomics in Globalization: Productivity, Wages, Profits, and Exchange Rates in an Era of Globalization." *Brazilian Journal of Political Economy* 22(85): 53–78.

Miozzo, Marcela. 2002. "Sectoral Specialisation in East Asia and Latin America Compared." *Brazilian Journal of Political Economy* 22(88): 48–68.

Nölke, Andreas. 2014. "Brazilian Corporations, the State and Transnational Activity: Introduction to the Special Issue." *Critical Perspectives in International Business* 10(4): 230–36.

Singal, Ajay, and Arun Kumar Jain. 2012. "Outward FDI Trends from India: Emerging MNCs and Strategic Issues." *International Journal of Emerging Markets* 7(4): 443–56.

Wang, Chengqi, Junjie Hong, Mario Kafouros, and Mike Wright. 2012. "Exploring the Role of Government Involvement in Outward FDI from Emerging Economies." *Journal of International Business Studies* 43(7): 655–76.

Wei, Yingqi, Xiaming Liu, Shengang Wang, and Jue Wang. 2012. "Local Sourcing of Multinational Enterprises in China." *International Journal of Emerging Markets* 7(4): 364–82.

CONCLUSION

Alden, Chris, and Maxi Schoeman. 2013. "South Africa in the Company of Giants: The Search for Leadership in a Transforming Global Order." *International Affairs* 89(1): 111–29.

Babones, Salvatore. 2011. "The Middling Kingdom: The Hype and the Reality of China's Rise." *Foreign Affairs* 90(5): 79–88.

Bardhan, Pranab. 2010. *Awakening Giants. Feet on Clay: Assessing the Economic Rise of China and India*. Princeton: Princeton University Press.

Beausang, Francesca. 2012. *Globalization and the BRICs. Why the BRICs Will Not Rule the World for Long*. Basingstoke: Palgrave Macmillan.

Cheru, Fantu, and Cyril Obi. 2010. *The Rise of China in India and Africa*. London: ZED Books.

Elsenhans, Hartmut. 2006. *Globalization between a Convoy Model and an Underconsumptionist Threat*. Münster: LIT Verlag.

Flemes, Daniel. 2009. "India - Brazil - South Africa (IBSA) in the New Global Order." *International Studies* 46(4): 401–21.

Lo, Vai Io, and Mary Hiscock. 2014. *The Rise of the BRICS in the Global Political Economy: Changing Paradigms*. Aldershot: Edward Elgar.

Virmani, Arvind. 2006. "World Economy, Geopolitics and Global Strategy: Indo-US Relations in the 21st Century." *Economic and Political Weekly* 41(43–44): 4601–12.

CPSIA information can be obtained
at www.ICGtesting.com
Printed in the USA
LVOW03s0818280717
542705LV00003B/27/P

9 780804 799898